Women's Chronology

Women's Chronology

A HISTORY
OF WOMEN'S
ACHIEVEMENTS

VOLUME 1:
4000 B.C.
to 1849

Peggy Saari, Tim & Susan Gall, Editors

U·X·L®

AN IMPRINT OF GALE

DETROIT · NEW YORK · TORONTO · LONDON

Women's Chronology: A History of Women's Achievements

Peggy Saari, and Tim and Susan B. Gall, Editors

Staff

Elizabeth Des Chenes, *U•X•L Developmental Editor*
Carol DeKane Nagel, *U•X•L Managing Editor*
Thomas L. Romig, *U•X•L Publisher*

Margaret Chamberlain, *Permissions Specialist*
Shalice Shah, *Permission Associate*

Shanna P. Heilveil, *Production Assistant*
Evi Seoud, *Assistant Production Manager*
Mary Beth Trimper, *Production Director*

Pamela A. E. Galbreath, *Senior Art Director*
Cynthia Baldwin, *Product Design Manager*

Linda Mahoney, *Typesetting*

Library of Congress Cataloging-in-Publication Data

Women's chronology: a history of women's achievements/
Timothy and Susan B. Gall and Peggy Saari, editors

   p. cm.
   Includes index.

   Contents: v. 1. 4000 B.C-1849—v. 2. 1850-present

   ISBN 0-7876-0660-X (set).   ISBN 0-7876-0661-8 (vol. 1)

                            ISBN 0-7876-0662-6 (vol. 2)

   1. Women—History—Chronology. 2. Chronology-Historical
I. Gall, Timothy L. II. Gall, Susan B. III. Saari, Peggy.
   HQ1122.W67 1997
   305.4'09—dc21   97-5028
   [B]   CIP

∞™ This book is printed on acid-free paper that meets the minimum requirements of American National Standard for Information Sciences– Permanence Paper for Printed Library Materials, ANSI Z39.48-1984.

Printed in the United States of America

10 9 8 7 6 5 4 3 2

Contents

Dr. Shirley Ann Jackson
(see entry dated 1973)

Volume 1

Volume 2

Reader's Guide

Women's Chronology: A History of Women's Achievements explores the role women from all walks of life have played in shaping events and movements from antiquity to the present. International in scope, *Women's Chronology* entries each highlight a significant social, political, educational, or cultural milestone that has had an impact on history. Entrants—whether historical figures such as Cleopatra, scientists such as Nobel-laureate Marie Curie, or artists such as painter Faith Ringgold—were chosen both for their accomplishments and their lasting influence.

Women's Chronology entries are arranged chronologically by year. Sidebar boxes examine events and issues related to the topic, while more than 120 black-and-white illustrations help enliven and explain the text. Both volumes contain an historical overview, timeline of important events, "words to know" section, and cumulative index.

Queen Lilliuokalani of Hawaii (see entry dated 1893)

Acknowledgments

Special thanks are due for the invaluable comments and suggestions provided by U•X•L's women's books advisors:

Annette Haley, High School Librarian/Media Specialist at Grosse Ile High School in Grosse Ile, Michigan; Mary Ruthsdotter, Projects Director of the National Women's History Project; Francine Stampnitzky, Children's/Young Adult Librarian at the Elmont Public Library in Elmont, New York; and Ruth Ann Karlin Yeske, Librarian at North Middle School in Rapid City, South Dakota.

Added thanks go to Stephen Allison and Kelly Druckenbroad for their research assistance.

Comments and Suggestions

We welcome your comments and suggestions for future editions of *Women's Chronology*. Please write: Editor, *Women's Chronology*, U•X•L, 835 Penobscot Bldg., Detroit, Michigan, 48226-4094; call toll free: 1-800-347-4253; or fax: 313-961-6347.

Introduction

The Ancient World (4000 B.C.–A.D. 499)

Knowledge about women prior to recorded history is limited to a relatively small amount of archaeological evidence. This evidence was found on the European continent and is thought to date back nearly 26,000 years. A clearer picture of women starts to emerge after the beginning of the Bronze Age (4000 B.C.), when the earliest known human civilization was developed. These ancient people, called the Sumerians, formed agricultural settlements in the valleys of the Tigris and Euphrates rivers in Mesopotamia. In 3000 B.C. they devised the first written alphabet, known as cuneiform, leaving pieces of their history for future generations of scientists to unravel. Women figured prominently in Sumerian society. The Sumerians worshiped female deities, or goddesses, and the first known female poet was the Sumerian priestess Enheduanna. In Babylonia the Hammurabi Code (c. 1792–1750 B.C.) gave women economic independence and equal status with their

Georgia O'Keeffe (see entry dated 1920)

husbands. They were allowed to own land and to pass their property on to their children.

Clay statues found in China and dating from 3000 B.C. indicate that the Chinese worshiped fertility goddesses. Ancient Chinese historians also referred to a "women's kingdom" that existed in southeastern Tibet during the prehistoric period. (Tibet, a region on the Asian continent, is located in southwestern China and borders India.) In this society women shared political power with male warriors. According to Greek legend, women warriors called Amazons ruled yet another kingdom in southwestern Tibet. By the time of recorded history Tibetan women had achieved equal status with men, including the freedom to divorce and to bear children without being married. Women and men shared property equally, and remarriage was common. Mahayana Buddhism, the Tibetan religion, considered the differences between men and women to be irrelevant. While Buddhist nuns could not study with monks, they did serve as advisors to nobles and government ministers, and many have been remembered for their spiritual accomplishments.

Considerably more evidence is available about women of the Egyptian empire (c. 2680-1000 B.C.). Pictures in Egyptian tombs portray aristocratic women as dancers, musicians, athletes, and priestesses. According to legal documents recovered from archaeological sites, women rented, owned, and inherited property, owned slaves, and sold goods. A queen, who was considered to have divine powers, was equal to a pharaoh (a male ruler), and the right to succeed the throne passed through the female line. Court women also helped promote scientific and cultural knowledge.

With the advent of Assyrian law between 1450 and 1250 B.C., women began losing their rights in the Middle East. Assyrian women had to wear veils in public, and they were strictly subordinated to (or under the authority of) their husbands. Similarly, women were considered inferior to men in Hebrew (Jewish) society. Limited to maintaining the home and instructing their children in Jewish traditions, women were not even allowed to worship alongside men in the synagogue; nor could they study the Talmud or Torah. Fathers had absolute authority over daughters, who later became the property of husbands. A Jewish woman could be divorced by her husband if she failed to bear children, but she herself had no right to divorce. Even though women were repressed in Jewish society, however, the Hebrew Bible contains stories of strong women who became leaders and judges.

Women had distinctly different positions in the two Greek states: Athens and Sparta. Most of the existing records of ancient Greece were left by the patriarchal (male-headed) Athenian upper class, which relegated women to a subservient position. Females were valued solely for their ability to have male children. Education was considered a privilege for Athenian women, and they were not allowed to participate in government or war. But there seem to have been exceptions, since some historical documents mention Athenian women who were scientists, philosophers, mathematicians, and teachers. Women enjoyed a small degree of independence in the religious sphere. They were free to become priestesses and join groups that worshiped the mother goddess Athena.

In Sparta women had more freedom. Their primary function was to give birth to warriors, so they were expected to undergo physical training in order to have strong children. Women lived apart from men and, if married, could be visited by their husbands only under cover of darkness, which was thought to increase desire and fertility. Spartan girls were educated along with boys and participated in athletic competitions. By 400 B.C. Spartan women had grown quite wealthy and were becoming conspicuous consumers. Whereas Athenian women could not own property, Spartan women owned a full two-thirds of the land in their city-state. Athenian commentators attributed Sparta's eventual decline to the influence of women in Spartan society.

Although Roman women were not segregated like some Athenian women, they were still defined by their membership in men's households: first the houses of their fathers and then the houses of their husbands. The chaste and virtuous (pure) wife was the ideal in Roman society. Because ancient Rome was almost constantly engaged in wars, many Roman noble-women became widows while they were in the prime of life. Scholars have speculated that this factor contributed to a rise in immorality among noblewomen. As the Roman nobility became fabulously wealthy and as the society absorbed the influence of eastern Hellenistic (Greek) culture, the rigid standards of morality in the Roman republic began to decline and ultimately collapsed.

After the centralization of state government began in India, the two highest Hindu classes gained power over the lower classes. As a result of the Laws of Manu, Indian women became totally subordinated to the adult males in their families. A woman had no role in choosing a husband, and she had no right to divorce—even though a man could readily rid himself of a wife who did not obey him. Women were unable to remarry if widowed, and for a time they even lacked property rights. Eventually, however, women were allowed to support themselves if they had no sons. Hindu law also established an unfathomable practice called *suttee,* or widow burning, which continued in India into the twentieth century.

Early Christianity and Islam (A.D. 30—1100)

In the early years of Christianity women took an active role in spreading the teachings of Jesus of Nazareth (Jesus Christ). While he was alive Jesus treated women as being equal to men, preaching directly to women and including them in stories to illustrate his views. After the crucifixion of Jesus (estimated to be the year A.D. 30), women became leaders and evangelists in the Christian church. The Roman empire almost immediately began trying to eradicate this new religion because it taught pacifism (an antiwar philosophy). By A.D. 400 more than 100,000 Christians had been persecuted by the Romans. Among them were women saints and martyrs (people who die for a cause to which they are strongly committed) who later became models of humility and strength in Christian literature.

When the Christian church was institutionalized, however, it was structured like a Jewish synagogue, having incorporated the patriarchal (male-centered) traditions of Greece and Rome. Women were once again subordinated to men. The New Testament promoted virginity as the ideal state for women—and as a means of controlling lust in men. Consequently many women became nuns and joined convents. After 400 B.C. monastic communities (houses for people who have taken religious vows, especially monks and nuns) were formed throughout Europe. Abbesses (female heads of convents) had significant power within the church for nearly 700 years. Nevertheless subordination of women in general remained a part of Christian doctrine for several centuries.

Islam was founded by the prophet Muhammad in the seventh century in an Arab region called Mecca. According to the Koran, the Muslim holy book, women were equal to men in their responsibilities to God. In Arab society at the time, however, women were still in a subservient position. Muhammad strove to improve the lives of women by outlawing the killing of female infants, allowing girls to be educated with boys, and giving more legal rights to married women. Nevertheless he held to the belief that wives should be obedient to their husbands and that single women were cursed (as were single men) and presented a threat to social order. Men took several wives, whom they could divorce for any reason. Men who violated (raped or otherwise assaulted) women were said to be punished in the afterlife, but unfaithful women were punished severely—usually by their husbands—on Earth. After Muhammad died in A.D. 632 women lost many of the rights they had gained. They could no longer worship in the mosque (the building used for worship by Muslims) and they could not travel alone on the annual pilgrimage to Mecca (the site to which pilgrims journeyed in the Islamic world). However, women did retain economic rights and remained dominant in the household.

The Middle Ages (A.D. 500—1600)

Historical documents provide more extensive information about the lives of women during the Middle Ages. In Europe most women were married as teenagers to men who were in their late twenties. Domestic life revolved around the institution of marriage, which was declared a sacrament by the Christian church. Only half of the women lived through the childbearing years, and nearly half of their children died in infancy. Girls served apprenticeships to tradesmen, and women participated in retail guilds, which gave them their own income and a protected craft. Many unmarried women were able to support themselves. In some countries women of the lower classes worked at the same jobs as men, but most working-class women assisted their husbands in one of several trades.

Women also played an important role in the arts during the Middle Ages. Noblewomen were educated in convents, where they learned to copy and decorate manuscripts. Nuns also ran prosperous workshops that produced some of the most beautifully illustrated manuscripts of the time. Another significant contribution of both noblewomen and nuns in the Middle Ages was the making of tapestries that commemorated religious and secular (or worldly) events. They also embroidered vestments and made panel paintings. Since the women usually worked in groups, the names of individual artists remain unknown. A few women even rose to the rank of scholar, producing books that provide valuable information about medieval life. Similarly, court ladies in Asian countries such as Japan and China became artists, writers, and performers.

In Europe, Asia, and Africa women of the royal class were prepared for ruling at an early age. Marriages for princesses were often arranged for political purposes at the time of the girl's birth; she was then educated along with her brothers to assume the responsibilities of power. Kings have traditionally been credited with major accomplishments in war and nation building, but many female regents and queens had long, productive reigns that contributed to the economic prosperity and cultural advancement of their countries. Throughout the Middle Ages certain women in European, Asian, and African countries became famous warriors, playing a significant role in defending or expanding their territories.

Near the end of the Middle Ages witchcraft hysteria swept across Europe, reaching the New England colonies in the seventeenth century. Although superstitions about heretical women (women who went against the teachings of the church) consorting with the devil had endured from ancient times, the Christian church—both Protestant and Catholic—started a witch-hunting campaign with women as their targets. In the late fifteenth century church authorities began printing hundreds of sensational tracts that gave instructions about how to identify witches. By the mid-sixteenth century people had become almost totally convinced of the power of witchcraft. Men were sometimes accused of practicing sorcery, but the main victims of witch-hunts were usually non-Christian lower-class widows who lived in rural areas. From 1480 until 1700 more than 100,000 people—75 percent of them women—were tried as witches, and a substantial number were executed.

The Early Modern World (1500–1799)

During the sixteenth century women of the working classes in Western Europe engaged in cottage industries, working for pay substantially lower than that of men. (Cottage industries are businesses comprised of laborers who work at home with their own equipment.) Nearly all women in the lower classes had little or no education, and they remained subservient to men. Educational opportunities for upper-class European women, however, began to increase with the Renaissance, the rebirth of classical learning.

The invention of the printing press also made more books available. Literacy among women was encouraged by Protestant churches so they could read the scriptures, and Catholic nuns founded religious orders for the education of girls. Women in wealthy families, who were taught by private tutors, became patrons (supporters) of great scholars; many engaged in scholarly pursuits themselves. Several women became well-known painters. In France ladies opened salons where the leading artists and intellectuals of the day discussed literature, science, and philosophy. These salons were instrumental in the development of the eighteenth-century Enlightenment movement, which promoted new systems of thought and art based on rationalism. (Rationalism is the reliance on reason and experience as the basis for truth.) As women engaged in intellectual pursuits such as composing novels and scientific treatises (written arguments on a given topic), debate about the place of women in society was rekindled.

In America women actively participated in the life of the emerging nation. Throughout the seventeenth-century English females as well as males signed contracts with colonists to work in the fields for four to seven years in exchange for passage to the New World. A few of the women married into wealthy families when they were freed, but most found servitude to be oppressive and their masters to be brutal. In the early eighteenth century the lifestyle of women depended on their class and race. By this time African American women had become integral to the economic success of many southern plantations. Wealthy white mistresses on these plantations oversaw as many as 20 household workers, a quarter of whom were indentured women. To the North, women among the middle and upper classes in the New England, Virginia, and Maryland colonies managed large estates and bought and sold land. Free-thinking women petitioned for the right to vote, many worked as doctors and lawyers, and several ran their own businesses. Some women in New England became writers and others were early advocates of education for all females.

The Industrialized World (1800—1899)

The Industrial Revolution (1750–1850) brought about profound social change in Europe, Britain, North America, and Asia. Throughout the world people were moving from rural areas to cities to work in factories and mills. Among those workers were women, who received low pay and labored long hours under poor conditions. At the same time, however, educational opportunities for middle-class women began to rise. In the United States coeducational schools were established in the early 1800s and teaching became the leading profession for women. As the level of education rose, women increased their involvement in social issues. Women abolitionists were instrumental in bringing an end to slavery during the American Civil War. In Western Europe, Britain, North America, and Japan, women campaigned for better conditions in factories and mills. By the end of the nineteenth century female activists were leading labor strikes, forming unions, and lobbying for labor reform laws. Women also established settlement houses for the poor, assisted in immigrant resettlement, founded philanthropic organizations, and trained nurses in improved hospital procedures.

An outgrowth of women's activism was the feminist movement, which began in the late 1840s and spread throughout the United States, Western Europe, Britain, and Japan. Women formed grass-roots organizations, held conventions, and lobbied governments in an effort to gain equality. They demanded equal legal status, property and inheritance rights, educational opportunities, and suffrage (the right to vote). Although feminists did not immediately win the vote, they were nevertheless instrumental in bringing about social and educational reform. By the end of the nineteenth century universal education was standard in nearly all the industrialized societies of the world. More and more women were attending college, and some entered professions previously open only to men, including law, medicine, and the sciences. Women were participating in the arts in greater numbers, becoming novelists, poets, painters, sculptors, dancers, singers, and musicians.

The Twentieth Century (1900–1997)

Women throughout the world remained at the forefront of social reform during the twentieth century, helping to gain new rights for themselves, for racial and ethnic minorities, for the underprivileged, and for the oppressed. During the early 1900s the suffragist movement intensified in all industrialized countries, reaching underdeveloped countries by mid-century. In the 1950s nearly every nation in the world had granted women the right to vote. Women's involvement in labor issues also continued into the twentieth century, as the world became increasingly industrialized. Intensifying work strikes and unionization efforts, they campaigned for the elimination of sweatshops, the outlawing of child labor, and the establishment of reasonable work hours. During World War I (1914-1918) women assisted in the war effort by volunteering as nurses, and when World

War II (1939-1945) broke out they replaced male workers in factories, businesses, and schools. Women continued to be active in pacifist (peace) movements during wars and conflicts since World War II, campaigning for an end to the draft in the 1960s and for nuclear disarmament in the 1970s through the 1990s.

Perhaps the most important development in the twentieth century was the "second wave" of feminism. Having begun in the nineteenth century, the women's movement reached a peak during civil rights and peace movements in the 1960s, particularly in the United States. By the 1980s women in Europe, Britain, North America, Asia, and some parts of Africa had gained access to most jobs, professions, and activities that had previously been the exclusive domain of men. Women were presidents, prime ministers, cabinet members, ambassadors, and members of governing bodies. They headed major corporations, led labor organizations, ran their own businesses, worked as stockbrokers, sold real estate, and managed factories. Women gained recognition as Nobel scientists, researchers, and inventors. They soared to new heights as athletes, astronauts, and explorers. Female participation increased dramatically in all areas of the arts as well, including film, theater, music, painting, and literature.

While women were still fighting political oppression in many parts of the world in the late 1990s, the gateways for female equality and advancement were opening wider than ever before in human history. And so the twentieth century will no doubt be remembered as "the women's century."

Photo Credits

The photographs appearing in *Women's Chronology: A History of Women's Achievements* were received from the following sources:

On the cover: Rosa Parks (**Courtesy of AP/Wide World Photos. Reproduced by permission.**); Mary Cassatt (**Courtesy of Archive Photos, Inc. Reproduced by permission.**); Nefertari (**Courtesy of Corbis-Bettmann. Reproduced by permission.**).

AP/Wide World Photos. Reproduced with permission.: pp. v, xi, 163, 208, 212, 224, 225, 229, 232, 238, 244, 249, 254, 257, 259, 260, 266, 268, 271, 273, 274, 275, 280, 282, 286, 291, 292, 296, 302, 305, 309, 320, 329, 332, 335, 338; **Corbis-Bettmann. Reproduced by permission.:** pp. vii, xix, xxv, 4, 6, 7, 11, 26, 34, 43, 64, 83, 84, 91, 131, 149, 157, 168, 186, 187, 199, 201, 253; **Archive Photos, Inc. Reproduced by permission.:** pp. xxi, 56, 166, 171, 205, 220, 231, 235, 263, 276, 307, 346, 351, 353; **UPI/ Corbis-Bettmann. Reproduced by permission.:** pp. 1, 93, 191, 213, 215, 223,

237, 245, 277, 311, 330; **The Granger Collection (New York City). Reproduced with permission.:** 19, 88, 98, 156; **The Bettmann Archive. Reproduced by permission.:** pp. 73, 230; **Courtesy of Library of Congress. Reproduced by permission.:** pp. 76, 129, 167, 218; **Archive Photos/Popperfoto. Reproduced by permission.:** pp. 85, 148, 234, 241; **Source unknown:** pp. 144, 151, 181; **National Portrait Gallery (London). Reproduced by permission.:** p. 161; **National Portrait Gallery (Washington, DC.). Reproduced by permission.:** pp. 164, 278; **Underwood & Underwood/Corbis-Bettmann. Reproduced by permission.:** p. 207; **University Research Library, UCLA. Reproduced by permission.:** p. 209; **The Oakland Museum, The City of Oakland (CA). Reproduced by permission.:** p. 247; **Courtesy of Chris Felver. Reproduced by permission.:** p. 347.

Women's Chronology: A Timeline of Events

4000-3500 B.C. According to Sumerian legend, the goddess Tiamet created the universe.

2640 B.C. Empress Si Long-shi originated silk-making in China.

c. 440 B.C. Esther saved the Jews.

c. 69 B.C. Egyptian queen Cleopatra was born.

A.D. 1137 Eleanor of Aquitaine inherited her father's lands.

A.D. 1429 Joan of Arc liberated Orleans, France, from English rule.

Eleanor of Aquitaine (see entry dated 1137)

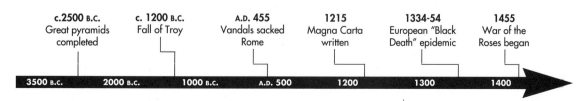

| c.2500 B.C. Great pyramids completed | c. 1200 B.C. Fall of Troy | A.D. 455 Vandals sacked Rome | 1215 Magna Carta written | 1334-54 European "Black Death" epidemic | 1455 War of the Roses began |

3500 B.C. 2000 B.C. 1000 B.C. A.D. 500 1200 1300 1400

1479	Queen Isabella began forming a united Spain.
1558	British Queen Elizabeth I took the throne.
1564	Maharanee Durgawati died at the Battle of Narhi.
1608	Midwife Louise Bourgeois wrote textbook on childbirth.
c. 1658	Marguerite Bourgeoys advanced religion and education in New France.
1677	Native American queen Cockacoeske endorsed the Treaty of Middle Plantation.
1691	Sor Juana Inés de la Cruz wrote an important feminist essay.
1718	Mary Montagu introduced smallpox vaccine to England.
c. 1720	Painter Rosalba Carriera introduced the use of pastels.
1762	Catherine the Great became ruler of Russia.
1837	Queen Victoria began ruling Great Britain.
1843	Sojourner Truth lectured about suffrage and abolition.
1848	The first "Woman's Rights Convention" was held in Seneca Falls, New York.
1852	Harriet Beecher Stowe wrote *Uncle Tom's Cabin*.
1854	Florence Nightingale introduced nursing innovations.
1856	Chinese "Dragon Empress" Cixi gained power.
1899	Senda Berenson wrote rules for women's basketball.
1905	Elizabeth Gurley Flynn cofounded the Industrial Workers of the World (IWW).

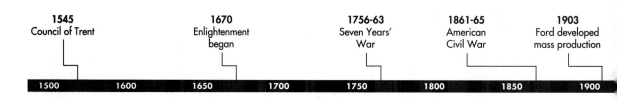

1545 Council of Trent

1670 Enlightenment began

1756-63 Seven Years' War

1861-65 American Civil War

1903 Ford developed mass production

1500   1600   1650   1700   1750   1800   1850   1900

1908	The International Olympic Committee gave official recognition to female athletes.
1912	Maria Montessori published *The Montessori Method.*
1913	Amy Lowell wrote Imagist verse.
1915	Lillian Gish appeared in the first modern film.
1924	Ichikawa Fusae led women's suffrage movement.
1925	Alice Evans pioneered milk pasteurization.
1927	Martha Graham founded dance company.
1932	Amelia Earhart flew across the Atlantic Ocean.
1935	Mary McLeod Bethune founded the National Council of Negro Women.
1938	Frances Moulton became bank president.
1940	Corrie ten Boom hid Jews from the Nazis.
1944	Hannah Senesh was executed.
1947	Anne Frank's diary published.
1949	Simone de Beauvoir published *The Second Sex.*
1950	Althea Gibson played in USLTA tournament.
1951	Marianne Moore won the Pulitzer Prize for poetry.
1952	Rosalind Franklin helped determine the structure of DNA.
1953	Queen Elizabeth II of England was crowned.
1955	Singer Marian Anderson appeared at the Metropolitan Opera.
1959	Ruth Handler created the Barbie Doll.
1962	Rachel Carson published *Silent Spring.*
1963	Katherine Graham took over the *Washington Post.*
1965	Jane Goodall founded chimpanzee research center.

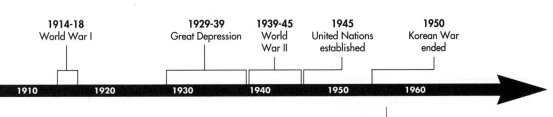

1914-18
World War I

1929-39
Great Depression

1939-45
World War II

1945
United Nations established

1950
Korean War ended

1910   1920   1930   1940   1950   1960

1965 Opera star Maria Callas retired.

1969 Golda Meir was elected prime minister of Israel.

1972 Gloria Steinem cofounded *Ms.* magazine.

1975 Dr. Helen Caldicott led the antinuclear movement.

1979 National Women's Hall of Fame dedicated.

1979 Margaret Thatcher became British prime minister.

1981 Sandra Day O'Connor was appointed U.S. Supreme Court Justice.

1982 Russian cosmonaut Svetlanta Saviskaya walked in space.

1984 Indian prime minister Indira Gandhi was assassinated.

1985 Wilma P. Mankiller became chief of the Cherokee Nation.

1986 Chemist Susan Solomon explained the "hole" in the ozone layer.

1988 Benazir Bhutto was elected prime minister of Pakistan.

1991 Anita Hill testified about sexual harrassment in televised Senate hearings.

1993 Janet Reno became U.S. attorney general.

1996 Astronaut Shannon Lucid spent 188 days in space.

1997 Madeleine Albright became the first female U.S. Secretary of State.

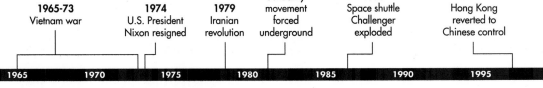

1965-73 Vietnam war

1974 U.S. President Nixon resigned

1979 Iranian revolution

1981 Solidarity movement forced underground

1986 Space shuttle Challenger exploded

1997 Hong Kong reverted to Chinese control

| 1965 | 1970 | 1975 | 1980 | 1985 | 1990 | 1995 |

Words to Know

Billie Holiday (see entry dated 1946)

A

Abbess: A woman who heads a convent of nuns.

Abolitionist: A person who advocates putting an end to slavery.

Abstractionism: A form of art that provides little or no realistic detail.

Aeronautical engineer: An engineer who designs aircraft.

Anatomist: A scientist who studies the structure of organisms such as the human body.

Aristocracy: Government by a privileged class of people.

Astronomer: A person who makes observations of objects and matter outside the earth's atmosphere.

B

Bacteriologist: A scientist who studies bacteria and their relationship to medicine, industry, and agriculture.

Biochemist: A scientist who studies chemical compounds and processes in living organisms.

Biologist: A scientist who studies plant and animal life.

Biophysicist: A scientist who applies physics to biological problems.

Bishop: Supervisor over clergymen in a religious organization.

Bluestocking: A woman having literary or intellectual interests.

Buddhism: A religion that grew out of the teachings of Gautama Buddha, who stressed that suffering can be overcome by mental and moral self-purification.

C

Cardinal: An official who ranks next below the pope in the Roman Catholic Church.

Cartographer: A map maker.

Cathedral: A church where a bishop resides.

Choreographer: A person who creates dance movements.

Christianity: A religion derived from the teachings of Jesus Christ.

Cinematographer: A motion picture cameraperson.

Classical: Relating to the ancient Greek and Roman world.

Communism: A theory advocating the elimination of private property.

Concerto: A musical piece for one or more soloists and orchestra with three contrasting movements.

Conservative: A political philosophy based on tradition and social stability, stressing established institutions, and preferring gradual rather than abrupt change.

Convent: A community or house of nuns belonging to a religious order or congregation.

Courtesan: A prostitute who has wealthy or upper-class clients.

Crusades: Military expeditions undertaken by the Christian church from the eleventh through the thirteenth centuries to win the Holy Land from the Muslims.

D

Democracy: A form of government in which the supreme power is held by the people and administered through representation.

Dynasty A succession of rulers from the same family.

E

Enlightenment: A philosophic movement of the eighteenth century marked by a rejection of traditional social, religious, and political ideas in favor of reason.

Epidemiologist: A medical scientist who studies the number and distribution of cases of disease within a population.

Exile: Forced absence from one's country or home.

F

Feminist: A person who supports the political, economic, and social equality of the sexes.

G

Geneticist: A biologist who studies the genetic makeup of organisms.

Geophysicist: A scientist who studies the physical properties of the earth and its environment.

H

Hinduism: The dominant religion of India that emphasizes using mystical contemplation and self discipline to reach a state of peace.

I

Immunologist: A scientist who studies the immune system of the human body.

Impressionism: A type of painting popular in the late nineteenth century characterized by the use bright colors to simulate reflected light on natural objects.

Islam: The religious faith of Muslims based on the belief in Allah as the sole deity and in Muhammad as his prophet.

J

Judaism: A religion developed among the ancient Hebrews based on the belief in one God who revealed himself to Abraham, Moses, and the Hebrew prophets. Followers advocate a religious life in accordance with the Scriptures and rabbinical traditions.

L

Liberalism: A political philosophy based on a belief in progress, the freedom of the individual, and the need for protection of political and civil liberties .

Lithographer: A person who etches images on stone or metal for printing with ink.

M

Marine biologist: A scientist who studies living organisms in oceans and seas.

Matriarchy: A family, group, or state headed by a woman, with descendence and inheritance determined by the female line.

Medieval: Pertaining to the Middle Ages, the period of European history from about A.D. 500 to about 1500.

Monastery: A residence for monks who have taken religious vows.

Monk: A man who belongs to a religious order.

Mysticism: The belief that direct knowledge of God, spiritual truth, or ultimate reality can be attained through personal experience.

Mythology: Stories and legends about gods, demigods, and heroes of a particular people.

N

Naturalist: A scientist who studies nature; a field biologist.

Nazism: Political, social, and economic doctrines held and put into effect by the National Socialist German Workers' party of the Third German Reich (1933-1945) which advocated total state control of government and industry.

Neurobiologist: A scientist who studies the nervous system.

Neuroendocrinologist: A scientist who studies the interaction between the nervous system and the endocrine system.

Neuropsychologist: A scientist who studies the influence of the nervous system on behavior.

Nun: A woman who belongs to a religious order.

O

Ornithologist: A scientist who studies birds.

P

Pacifism: Opposition to war or violence as a means of settling disputes; also the refusal to bear arms on moral or religious grounds.

Pagan: A person who worships many gods.

Patriarchal: Social organization characterized by the supremacy of the father in the family or clan, with wives and children acting as dependents. In patriarchal groups, descent and inheritance are determined by the male line.

Pharaoh: A ruler—usually male—of ancient Egypt.

Physicist: A scientist who studies the interaction between energy and matter.

Pope: The bishop of Rome and the head of the Roman Catholic Church.

Prehistoric: Existing in a time before recorded history.

Priestess: a woman authorized to perform the sacred rites of a religion.

Primatologist: A scientist who studies apes, monkeys, and other animals such as lemurs.

Prime minister: The chief minister of a ruler or a state.

Psychologist: A scientist who studies the human mind and behavior.

R

Regent: A person who governs a kingdom in the place of sovereign who is a minor or who is absent or disabled.

Renaissance: The transition movement between medieval and modern times, beginning in Italy in the fourteenth century and lasting into the seventeenth century; a period marked by a revival of classical arts and literature and the beginnings of modern science.

Revolution: The violent overthrow of one government or ruler and the substitution of another by those who are governed.

Roman Catholicism: The faith, practice, and system of the ancient Christian church.

S

Saint: One who has been officially recognized by a religious group as being holy.

Salon: An assemblage of intellectuals, literary figures, artists, and statesmen in the home of a prominent hostess.

Words to Know

Shinto: The principal religion of Japan, Shinto is based on a devotion to nature-based deities (gods and goddesses) and worship of the emperor as the descendent of the Sun goddess.

Shrine: A place in which devotion is paid to a saint or deity.

Socialism: A political and economic theory advocating collective or governmental ownership and administration of the production and distribution of goods.

Suffrage: The right to vote.

Suffragette: A woman who advocates the right to vote for women.

T

Temperance: Advocacy of moderation in, or abstinence from, the use of alcoholic beverages.

W

Witchcraft: The use of magic or sorcery (power gained from the assistance or control of evil spirits).

Z

Zoologist: A biologist who studies and classifies animal life.

The Chronology

c. 4000—3500 B.C. ▪ Tiamat ruled Sumerian gods

Tiamat was the ruler of all the gods of the people of ancient Sumer (now southern Iraq). According to the "Akkadian Epic" (a long poem written in the Akkadian language around 1000 B.C.), the god of fresh water, Apsu, impregnated Tiamat, the goddess of ocean (salt) water. From this union came other gods who lived in Tiamat's belly. She ruled over all the gods, including Apsu, until a civil war broke out across the land. As the legend goes, when the young hero god Marduk accused Tiamat of being too haughty (acting arrogant or overly self-important), she opened her mouth to devour him. At that moment Marduk sent a whirlwind into her belly, then killed her with an arrow. Splitting Tiamat's corpse in two, Marduk is said to have used its parts to create the universe.

c. 3500 B.C. ▪ Eurynome created the universe

The Pelasgians, the earliest inhabitants of Greece, believed the world was created by Eurynome, the goddess of

Women's Roles in Ancient Egypt

Drawings on Old Kingdom (c. 2680–2258 B.C.) tombs and monuments indicate that women dancers and musicians were common in ancient Egypt. Women of a wealthy household were often depicted entertaining their husbands and fathers with music. Some women were named as overseers of musical troupes during this time. Women are also shown delivering cloth and receiving payment, and there are records of women having the title "overseer of weavers" or "overseer of the house of weavers" who were part of a large household and were probably servants or slaves. Another occupation for women was that of professional mourner.

Legal documents reflect that male officials of the upper class in Egypt could inherit property from their mothers, and women could inherit property from their husbands. In the Middle Kingdom (c. 2000–1786 B.C.) inheritance passed to the son of a rich man's daughter, not directly to a son. Egyptian daughters were sometimes called a name that translates as "ruler of her father" or "beautiful as her father."

all things. When Eurynome rose from the waters of Chaos (a vast, empty space), she divided it into sky and sea and danced upon the waves. The north wind created by her dance turned into the serpent Ophion, which impregnated her. Taking the form of a dove, Eurynome then laid the Universal Egg, and Ophion coiled seven times around the egg until it hatched in two. Out of the egg tumbled all the things in the universe: sun, moon, planets, stars, mountains, rivers, trees, animals, and humans.

c. 3000 B.C. ▪ Chinese worshipped fertility deities

Clay statues unearthed in the Liaoning province in northern China provide images of Chinese women in the Neolithic period (New Stone Age). Dating from about 3000 B.C., these large-breasted figures were probably fertility deities worshiped by the ancient Chinese to guarantee that children would be born and crops would grow.

Egyptian Goddesses

Hathor and Neith were only two of many goddesses in Egyptian myths. The most important was Isis, Mistress of Magic and Speaker of Spells, who gained power over Ra, the sun god. Isis was the wife of Osiris—a fertility god and later King of the Dead—and the mother of the Horus, the first Egyptian king. She is remembered as the symbolic mother of all Egyptian kings. Maat was the goddess of truth, justice, and law. Sekhmet, the daughter of Ra, guarded her father's boat as it passed through the twelve zones of the afterworld. She later became a lion goddess associated with hunting. Other cat and lion goddesses included Bastet, Tefnut, Mekhit, Nafdet, and Mut, whose cults (the term "cult" refers to a system of worship and those who follow it) thrived when lions and panthers roamed Egypt. Also important were the snake goddesses Wadjet, Meretseger, and Renenutet. Major deities associated with childbirth were Meskhenet, Taweret, and Bes, while Isis, Neith, Nephthys, and Serkhet were concerned with death and burial.

2800 B.C. ▪ Mer-Nei ruled Egypt alone

The Great Royal Heiress Mer-Nei, who became ruler of Egypt in 2800 B.C., was the first queen to reign alone over her kingdom. Her tombs at Saqqara and Abydos equaled the tombs of kings in both size and splendor.

2700 B.C. ▪ Merit Ptah was earliest female doctor

Merit Ptah was the earliest known female doctor. She is depicted on a tomb in the Valley of the Kings in Egypt.

c. 2680 B.C. ▪ Egyptian goddesses Hathor and Neith

The title "priestess of Hathor" was common among upper-class women during the Old Kingdom (c. 2680–2258 B.C.) in Egypt. Hathor was the sky and cow goddess as well as the goddess of the dead. She was also a fertility goddess who represented the seven fates that could foretell a child's future at birth. Priestesses of Neith represented the national goddess of Lower Egypt, who created all things and was worshiped from

the beginning of Egyptian history. The goddess of hunting and war, she was never paired with a male god. Many early queens took her name.

2640 B.C. ▪ Si Ling-shi originated silk-making

The empress of China, Si Ling-Shi, is credited with developing the process for removing thread from the cocoon of

Minoan-Mycenean Goddesses

Around 2000 B.C. the Aryans from Russia and Turkistan invaded the Aegeans (Pelasgians) and the Minoans of Crete (an island in the Mediterranean Sea).They formed the Minoan-Mycenean civilization, which flourished from 1600 B.C. to 1400 B.C. and became what is now considered Greek culture. Greek mythology included numerous goddesses that played important but complex roles. Hera, for example, was queen of the gods; she is believed to have resided on Mount Olympus. The sister and wife of the supreme god Zeus, Hera served as the protector of women and presided over marriage and childbirth. Demeter, the goddess of the harvest and fertility, was honored at Athens in a fertility festival attended only by women. Rhea, a Titan (principal deity or chief goddess), was the mother of Zeus, Poseidon (god of the sea), Hestia (goddess of the hearth), Hera, and Demeter. Another major deity was Athena, who served many functions: goddess of war and peace, arts and crafts, and wisdom, as well as guardian of cities. Aphrodite was the goddess of fertility, love, and beauty; she was also worshiped as a sea goddess, a war goddess, and the patron of sailors.

the silk worm. She started silk cultivating and weaving industries in 2640 B.C.

2300 B.C. ▪ Enheduanna praised the goddess Inanna

The Sumerian priestess Enheduanna was the first known female poet. In 2300 B.C. she composed "Exaltation of Inanna" in praise of Inanna, the fertility goddess and the goddess of the Sacred Marriage, who had been worshiped in Sumeria since 3000 B.C. Inanna is said to have descended to the underworld in search of Dumuzi, her mortal lover and husband. The story of Inanna and Dumuzi was later written in two other Sumerian compositions, "Inanna's Descent to the Netherworld" and "Dumuzi's Dream." (c. 1765 B.C.)

c. 2200—2101 B.C. ▪ Semiramis founded Babylon

The mythical Assyrian queen Semiramis, who conquered many lands, founded the city of Babylon in Mesopotamia.

Queen Nefertari of Egypt was made a goddess after her death.

Constructing the first known tunnel below a river, she linked the royal palace with the Temple of Jupiter by tunnel under the Euphrates. Semiramis vanished from the earth in the shape of a dove and was worshiped as a deity (a god or goddess) who had characteristics of Ishtar, the Akkadian goddess of love .

1570 B.C. ▪ Nefertari known as "god's wife"

Queen Ahmose Nefertari was the sister and principal wife of King Ahmose of Egypt during the Eighteenth Dynasty, which marked the beginning of the New Kingdom. (c. 1570 to 1305 B.C.) During their reign Ahmose enacted a law creating the position of "god's wife of Ahmun" for Nefertari and her heirs because she preferred the title "god's wife" to "king's wife." Nefertari participated in temple rituals along with male priests and advised her husband on various building projects. Outliving both her husband and her son, she was deified (made into a goddess) and worshiped throughout the New Kingdom.

1570 B.C. ▪ Ahhotep ruled with her son

During the rule of King Ahmose of Egypt, an Asiatic people called Hyksos invaded northern Egypt and controlled Nubia, an area south of Egypt. Ahmose succeeded in driving the Hyksos out of both the northern and the southern territories. His eulogy (written or spoken tribute to the dead) to his mother, Queen Ahhotep, suggests that she ruled Egypt with him. The inscription reads: "One who cares for Egypt. She has looked after Egypt's soldiers. She has guarded her [meaning the land of Egypt]. She has brought back her fugitives [runaways] and collected together her deserters. She has pacified [made peaceful] Upper Egypt and expelled her rebels."

Queen Hatshepsut ruled
Egypt after the death
of Thutmose II around
1490 B.C.

c. 1490 B.C. ▪ Hatshepsut became king of Egypt

Queen Hatshepsut was the daughter of Thutmose I of Egypt and half-sister and wife of Thutmose II, with whom she began ruling in 1488 B.C. When Thutmose II died around 1490 B.C., Hatshepsut ruled in the place of her half-brother, Thutmose III, who was still a child. During the second year of her reign, the god Amun appeared to Hatshepsut in his temple at

Muses Provide Intellectual Inspiration

Greek goddesses called the Muses—the daughters of the supreme god Zeus and the goddess of memory Mnemosune—resided on Mount Helikon. As the source of all knowledge, the Muses were called upon by poets when they sang. Originally three Muses exercised various powers, but over time the number evolved to nine, with each operating in a particular area of the arts and sciences: Calliope (epic poetry), Clio (history), Erato (love poetry), Euterpe (lyric poetry), Melpomene (tragedy), Polyhymnia (sacred poetry), Terpsichore (choral song and dance), Thalia (comedy), and Urania (astronomy).

Thebes. According to a stela (inscribed stone slab) found at Karnak, Amun crowned her the King of Two Lands. Hatshepsut also took several other titles, including the Daughter of Ra and Khunum-et-Amun Hatshepsut, which allied her directly with the gods. Formally called king, she reportedly wore men's clothing; scribes even referred to her using male pronouns. Although Hatshepsut and Thutmose III ruled together, she was clearly the dominant partner.

1405 B.C. ▪ Queen Tiy of Egypt depicted as king

Amenhotep III (1405–1367 B.C.) ruled at the height of Egyptian power and prosperity. Although his wife, Queen Tiy, was not of royal parentage, she is depicted in a colossal statue as being equal with the king. In a tomb scene Tiy is also shown sitting on the arm of a sphinx (a mythical beast with the head of a human and the body of a lion) that resembles her. She is warding off enemies, an act usually associated with a king.

Tiy was apparently the first queen to adopt as part of her insignia (a badge of authority or honor) the horns of the goddess Hathor. She also used the solar disk of Ra, the sun god, thus identifying herself with the cult of the sun. (*Also see entry dated c. 2680 B.C.: Egyptian goddesses Hathor and Neith.*)

1300 B.C. ▪ Miriam sang at parting of the Red Sea

Miriam was the sister of Moses, the Hebrew lawgiver, and Aaron, Moses' spokesperson in Egypt. After Moses miraculously parted the Red Sea (also known as the Sea of Reeds) and led the Hebrews out of Egypt into Canaan (the coastal areas of modern Israel and Syria), Miriam sang a song of praise with the Hebrew women, whom she herself had led. The Song of Miriam was one of the earliest pieces of Hebrew poetry. Later siding with Aaron against Moses, Miriam was stricken with leprosy (a contagious disease that deforms the body), but she was said to have been cured when Moses prayed for her.

c. 1200 B.C. ▪ Empress Fu Hao led military expeditions

Fu Hao was a consort (associate ruler) of the Emperor Wu Ding, who reigned in China from about 1200 to 1180 B.C. during the Shang dynasty. She led her people's armies on military expeditions, and it is known from the splendor of her tomb (which contains sacrificial victims, thousands of cowrie (marine life) shells, and hundreds of bronze and jade objects) that she was held in high esteem.

1200 B.C. ▪ Poet Phautasia inspired Homer

The Egyptian poet Phautasia, the daughter of Nicanchus of Memphis, composed poems about the Trojan War (a legendary conflict between the Greeks and the Trojans of ancient Turkey) and the Greek hero Odysseus (Ulysses). According to some scholars, the famous Greek poet Homer copied substantial portions of his *Iliad* and *Odyssey* from Phautasia's poems.

The Myth of the Amazons

The Amazons were a mythical race of warrior superwomen who came from Libya and Scythia, an area in the steppes (treeless plains) of Russia. According to Greek mythology, they headed a matrilineal society in which women governed and waged wars while men performed household tasks. Before an Amazon could marry she had to kill a man, and her male children were said to be either killed or maimed at birth. A popular legend holds that the Amazons amputated one of their breasts (Amazon means "one breast") so they could shoot with bows and throw their spears more easily. Vase paintings and statues, however, show no evidence of this practice. The Amazons are believed to have been the first to use cavalry (armies fighting on horseback), and they were famous for numerous conquests throughout Asia Minor and Greece, where they fought against the great Greek heroes.

1187 B.C. ▪ Penthesilea died in battle

Penthesilea was queen of the Amazons, a mythical race of superwomen. During the siege of Troy the Trojan hero Hector was killed by Achilles, leader of the invading Myrmidons. When Penthesilea and her troops came to the aid of the Trojans, she was also slain by Achilles. He was so taken by her beauty and courage, however, that he fell in love with her dead body. According to the Roman scholar Pliny the Elder, Penthesilea was the inventor of the battle ax.

1183 B.C. ▪ Helen's kidnapping caused war

According to classic Greek myth the Spartan queen Helen was kidnapped sometime around 1180 B.C. by the Trojan prince Paris. Helen's husband, King Menelaus, amassed his troops and set out to take her back, thus beginning the Trojan War. In other versions, however, Helen was a goddess who chose her own king (Menelaus) but then later ran off with another lover (Paris). Because Menelaus could neither be king nor immortal without Helen's backing, he waged the war to regain his throne and his immortality.

1150 B.C. ▪ Deborah led tribes of Israel

Deborah was a prophetess and judge of Israel, the only woman to hold that position. She rallied (joined together for a common cause) the northern tribes (Issachar, Zebulon, and Naphtali) and the southern tribes (Ephraim, Benjamin, and Machir-Mannasseh) of Israel to defeat the invading Canaanite king Jabin. The result was several decades of peace. The Song of Deborah in the Hebrew Bible is considered one of the oldest surviving pieces of biblical writing.

853 B.C. ▪ Queen Jezebel introduced idol worship

After defeating the Assyrians at the Battle of Karkar in 853 B.C., King Ahab of Israel increased his power by marrying Jezebel, the daughter of King Ethbaal of the Phoenician cities of Tyre and Sidon. Ahab established his new capital at the city of Samaria in Canaan, which was the Promised Land of the Israelites. During Ahab's reign Jezebel introduced the worship of the Phoenician idols Baal and Asherah to the people of Israel. (Baal was the chief deity, whose functions included being the source of life and fertility as well as the lord of war. Asherah was the Great Mother goddess.) Jezebel's action enraged the prophet Elijah, whose mission was to wipe out idol worship and gain support for Yahweh, the One God of Israel.

811—807 B.C. ▪ **Queen Sammuramat ruled Assyrians**

Upon the death of King Shamshi-Adad V of Assyria, Queen Sammuramat, known also as the mythical Semiramis, became regent (substitute ruler) for her son Adadnirari. Records show that Sammuramat actually held the power, and during her five years as regent she introduced the worship of

Deborah rallied the tribes of Israel against the Canaanites.

the Babylonian god Nebo to Assyria. (*Also see entry dated c. 2200–2101 B.C.: Semiramis founded Babylon.*)

c. 753 B.C. ▪ Acca Laurentia fostered Romulus and Remus

According to legend, Rome was founded on a hilltop above the Tiber River by two infant brothers, Romulus and Remus. They had been placed in a basket by King Amulius of Alba Longa and set adrift on the river. After floating safely to shore they were nursed by a she-wolf until they were adopted by Acca Laurentia and her husband, a shepherd named Faustulus. In another version of the tale Acca Laurentia was actually a wealthy courtesan (a prostitute who had rich clients) who left all her money to the people of Rome. Since the Latin word for both "she-wolf" and "prostitute" is *lupus,* some scholars believe Romulus and Remus were not suckled by a she-wolf but were adopted immediately by Acca Laurentia. For a long period Acca Laurentia's death was commemorated on February 15 in a fertility festival called Lupercalia. During the festival girls would leave love messages in urns and boys would draw them out. Centuries later Lupercalia would be celebrated on February 14 as St. Valentine's Day.

c. 712 B.C. ▪ The *Kojiki*

According to the *Kojiki* ("Chronicle of Ancient Things"), the male deity Izanagi no Mikoto and the female deity Izanami no Mikoto created Japan and all other deities. The pair is said to have descended from the heavens, after which Izanami gave birth to the Japanese islands, with their deities of mountains, rivers, trees, and crops. In giving birth to the fire deity, Izanami burned and died.

c. 712 B.C. ▪ Amaterasu o Mikami, Shinto sun goddess

The goddess Amaterasu o Mikami (translated as "grand divinity illuminating heaven") was the principal Shinto deity.

The Lives of Vestal Virgins

Six Vestal Virgins held a special place in Roman society. Chosen for this role before they entered puberty, the vestals took a vow to remain chaste (not to engage in sexual intercourse) for thirty years. They tended the sacred fire in the Temple of Vesta (Greek: Hestia) and were allowed to appear in public. However, if anyone touched their chair as they were being carried in the street, that person was put to death. Once a year in a special ceremony, the vestals sacrificed and burned a pregnant heifer (a young cow that has not yet had offspring), using the ashes to wash and purify the temple. During this ceremonial time it was considered unlucky for couples to enter into marriage.

The vestals could be punished only by the chief priest, who might be required to whip an offender for breaking one of several strictly enforced rules. If a vestal were discovered to have broken the all-important vow of chastity, however, her punishment was to be buried alive.

(Shinto, Japan's oldest religion, centered on the belief in divine spirits, their interaction with humans, and the importance of the worship of nature.) Identified with the sun as ruler of the heavens and the origin of the Japanese imperial line (or ruling family), Amaterasu is enshrined in the Grand Shrine of Ise. The *Kojiki* ("Chronicle of Ancient Things") depicts her as the most positive of the three deities born to the creator deities, Izanami and Izanagi. She is said to have taught her subjects to plant rice and weave cloth.

c. 610 B.C. ▪ Sappho wrote poetry

The renowned Greek poet Sappho lived at Mytilene on the island of Lesbos, Greece. Founder of a boarding school for wealthy young women, she taught poetry, music, and social graces to prepare her students for marriage. Sappho was also the priestess of a cult, or religious following, dedicated to Aphrodite, the Greek goddess of love; this cult celebrated the love of women for one another. Only papyrus fragments of her seven or nine books—the origin of the term "lesbian" (for her

Spartan Women Exert Power

Girls and women in Sparta, the powerful city-state of ancient Greece, were the freest and most independent of all women in the ancient world. Like boys, girls were required to complete a standard course of education. The young women participated in athletics (notably races dedicated to the goddess Hera), wearing short chitons (tunics) similar to those worn by the legendary Amazons (famous female warriors). The victors were honored with statues of themselves on which their names were inscribed. This practice contrasted with the Athenian custom of naming a woman only in relation to a man (i.e., "the wife of Socrates," "the sister of Plato"). Greek philosopher Aristotle reported that girls and boys danced nude in processions (ceremonial gatherings, almost like parades) without embarrassment or concerns about modesty and proper behavior. He also indicated that two-thirds of the land in Sparta was owned by women.

island home)—have survived. Her poems have also been quoted by other writers. Sappho is considered one of the greatest poets of all time. The poetic meter called the "sapphic" was named for her, and she influenced other ancient poets.

600 B.C. ▪ Ishtar, Assyrian goddess of love

By 600 B.C. Ishtar had become the goddess of love in the Assyrian empire, the region surrounding the Tigris River in the Middle East. She was believed to be so powerful in the Assyrian city of Ninevah that her statue was sent to Egypt to help cure an ailing king.

c. 534 B.C. ▪ The "Street of Crime"

According to Roman historian Livy, the wife of Tarquinius Superbus (Tarquin the Proud) urged her husband to make himself king by killing her own father. After the murder she rode in an open carriage to the Roman Senate, loudly proclaiming Tarquin king. When the driver stopped the carriage because he saw her father's bloody body lying in the street, she grabbed the reins and drove over the corpse. As a result of this incident the street came to be called the Street of Crime. The evil deeds of Tarquin and his family, culminating in the rape of Lucretia by his son Sextus, are said to have caused the overthrow of the Tarquin dynasty and led to the founding of the Roman Republic. (*Also see entry dated c. 510 B.C.: The rape of Lucretia.*)

c. 510 B.C. ▪ The rape of Lucretia

In Italy during the sixth century B.C., Lucretia, the wife of Lucretius Tarquinius Collatinus, was raped by Sextus, the son of Tarquinius Superbus (Tarquin the Proud, head of the Etruscan dynasty of western-central Italy). At that time in history, victims of rape were often driven by their feelings of shame to take drastic and senseless action—and end their own lives. Lucretia reportedly summoned her family and stabbed herself in their presence. Popular outrage at her death sparked a revolution that, two years later, resulted in the expulsion of the Tarquin dynasty and the creation of the Roman Republic. Lucretia's husband and her uncle, Lucius Junius Brutus, were prominent revolutionaries and served as early leaders of the new government.

508 B.C. ▪ Cloelia depicted as statue

The ancient Romans left few representations of mortal women, whether in coins, statues, and paintings. However, ancient records refer to a girl named Cloelia, who earned the honor of being depicted by a statue. According to legend, Cloelia and other noble Roman girls were abducted by the Etruscans, people who migrated to Italy from Lydia, which is now Turkey, in the twelfth century B.C. Cloelia persuaded some of her companions to escape with her from their captors by swimming across the Tiber River. As they swam to safety, the Etruscans pelted them with stones and spears. The girls eventually reached Rome and were reunited with their families.

480 B.C. ▪ Artemisia I outwitted the Greeks

Artemisia I was the queen of the ancient city-state of Halicarnassus (in present-day Turkey). In 480 B.C. she advised the Persian ruler Xerxes not to engage the Greeks in a naval battle at Salamis (the chief city on the island of Cyprus). Commanding a fleet of over 1,000 vessels, however, Xerxes attacked 400 Greek ships at Salamis. Once the battle began Artemisia assisted Xerxes, outwitting the enemy with a force of her own warships. Artemisia was one of the few survivors on the Persian side. Outraged that a woman would presume to make war on them, the Greeks offered 10,000 drachmas (silver coins) for her capture. After Artemisia successfully fought them off, Xerxes is said to have commented, "My men have behaved like women and my women like men."

c. 440 B.C. ▪ Esther saved the Jews

The Book of Esther in the Old Testament of the Bible tells the story of the beautiful Jewish woman Esther, who was orphaned as a child and raised by her cousin Mordecai. Esther was chosen by the Persian king Ahasuerus (Xerxes) to replace his wife, Vashti, whom he had banished for disobeying him. (According to some accounts Vashti was executed.) King Ahasuerus had conquered the Egyptians and was attempting to overtake the Greeks and extend his empire from modern-day India to northern Africa. Mordecai, who served as a palace attendant after Esther assumed her place in the Persian empire, advised Esther to conceal her Jewish origin from King Ahasuerus. Later, one of the king's advisors, Haman, obtained an edict requiring all palace servants to bow down to him; Mordecai refused to obey. Haman then decreed that all Jews—men, women, and children—be murdered during Adar, the last month of the Hebrew year.

At this point Esther revealed her Jewish identity to Ahasuerus and exposed Haman's plot to kill the Jews. Upon learning of Haman's plan, King Ahasuerus ordered that he be executed. Ahasuerus then appointed Mordecai as his advisor. Esther's action in saving her people is commemorated by modern-day Jews in the festival of Purim.

352 B.C. ▪ Artemisia II ruled Caria

Artemisia II (?–350 B.C.) ascended to the throne of Caria (in present-day Aydin, Turkey) upon the death of her husband in 352 B.C. Becoming a powerful leader, she put down a rebellion by the inhabitants of the island of Rhodes (now a part of Greece). Artemisia also gained fame as a botanist (one who studies plants) and as a medical researcher.

300 B.C. ▪ Queen Medb of Ireland led cattle raid

The famous ancient Irish epic the *Táin Bó Cualigne* ("The Cattle Raid of Cooley") tells the story of Queen Medb (Maeve), who may have been an actual historical figure. She has also been identified as the goddess of sovereignty (supreme power) of Connacht (one of the provinces of Ire-

Ancient Irish Goddesses Oversee Warfare

Among the most prominent goddesses in ancient Ireland were Dana and Morrigan. Dana was a mother goddess of the Tuatha Dé Danann, a tribe in ancient Ireland. According to legend, the Dé Danann (also Danaan) were defeated by the Milesians, invaders from Spain and ancestors of present-day inhabitants of Ireland. Driven underground, the Dé Danann lived in mounds called *sídhe* and came to be known as *aes sídhe* ("people of the hills"), or fairies. The best-known is the banshee (*bean sídhe*), the female fairy whose wailing is said to warn a family of the death of one of its members.

Morrigan (also Morrighán) was the triune (consisting of three parts) goddess of war, death, and slaughter. Various meanings of her name include "great queen" and "phantom queen." She appeared as Badb ("crow" or "raven"), Nemhain ("frenzy"), and Macha. Each of these goddesses took the shape of a crow or raven with supernatural powers and helped the Tuatha Dé Danann in battle. The goddesses did not engage in armed conflict themselves but instead hovered above the battlefield as hooded crows, using their magic to strike terror in the enemy.

land). According to the tale, the White Horned Bull of Connacht had been born into Medb's herd, but—not wanting to be owned by a woman—it ran away to another herd. A jealous Medb learned of the Brown Bull of Cualigne in Ulster (another province) and, wanting it for her own, convinced her husband, Aillil, to help her raise an army to invade Cualigne and capture the bull. Medb's troops were ultimately defeated by the Ulster men, led by the hero Cúchulainn.

250 B.C. ▪ Athena was goddess of craftsmen and pilots

According to Greek myth, Athena came full-grown from the forehead of her father, Zeus, the creator of life. Zeus had swallowed his pregnant wife, Metis, then developed a headache. Athena was born when Zeus was struck on the head by an ax. She became a warrior and the supreme judge of Athens, a Greek city-state. The inventor of practical intelligence, she inspired potters, weavers, and other craftsmen. She also guided ship pilots safely through their sea journeys. Athena is said to have presided over life in Athens throughout the third century B.C.

250 B.C. ▪ Sul, the patron of Aquae Solis

Sul (Sulis) was a Celtic goddess identified with the Roman goddess Minerva, who governed arts and crafts, and the Greek goddess Athena, who performed a similar function. Sul was a patron of the natural hot-water springs located in present-day southwestern England. In the first century A.D. the Romans founded a city near the spring, calling it Aquae Solis ("waters of the sun," which is now known as the city of Bath). At Aquae Solis the Romans built baths and a temple that remained in use until the fourth century A.D. Excavated in 1755 and subsequently restored, the baths are now visited by thousands of people each year. (*Also see entry dated 250 B.C.: Athena, goddess of craftsmen and pilots.*)

c. 200 B.C. ▪ Lu Hou ruled Han dynasty

Empress Lu Hou was the wife of Gao Zu, the founding emperor of the Han dynasty (an early Chinese ruling family) in China, who reigned from 202 B.C. until his death in 195 B.C. After he died their son was named emperor, but Lu Hou was the actual ruler. Although a number of child emperors subsequently occupied the throne, she continued to hold considerable influence until rival factions (competing groups) had her killed in 180 B.C. Later Chinese historians vilified her (spoke evil of her), in part because of her ruthlessness in eliminating her enemies and also because they thought she violated the proper norms of female behavior.

80 B.C. ▪ Hsiang wrote biographies of women

Liu Hsiang was a Chinese author and civil servant who wrote *Biographies of Famous Women*. It is considered one of the first collections of biographies of women.

According to legend, Cleopatra used her beauty and power of persuasion to expand Egypt's power.

c. 69 B.C. ▪ Cleopatra was born

The daughter of Ptolemy XI of Egypt, Cleopatra married her younger brother, Ptolemy XII, when she was seventeen. They shared the throne at Alexandria, the capital of Egypt. Soon revealing her ambition for power, Cleopatra obtained the support of the Roman ruler Julius Caesar and led a revolt against her husband-brother. The coup was a success; Egypt

The Cult of Isis

The most powerful of the ancient Egyptian goddesses was Isis, Mistress of Magic and Speaker of Spells, who gained power over the sun god Ra. She was the wife of Osiris, a fertility god who later became King of the Dead. Isis had a son, Horus, the first Egyptian king, so she became the symbolic mother of all Egyptian kings—and was eventually known as the universal goddess. In about 80 B.C. worship of Isis reached Rome, where it flourished for four centuries before being overtaken by Christianity. Isis is said to have become Christianized through the cult of the Virgin Mary. Early Christians called themselves *Pastophori,* or "servants of Isis," which became the word "pastors."

then remained under the control of the Romans. After her husband was drowned in the Nile River, Cleopatra married another of her younger brothers, Ptolemy XIII, in 51 B.C. He deposed her (removed her from the throne) two years later, but Caesar restored her to the throne in 48 B.C.

By this time Cleopatra had become Caesar's mistress, and she followed him to Rome. She bore his son Caesarion, who would become Ptolemy XIV. When Caesar was murdered in 44 B.C., Cleopatra returned to Alexandria, arranged the murder of her former husband (and brother, Ptolemy XIII), and ruled with her son Ptolemy XIV. In 42 B.C. Cleopatra met Roman orator and general Marc Antony, who immediately fell in love with her. Reportedly hoping to use Antony to restore Egypt to its former power, Cleopatra married him in 36 B.C. The marriage made Antony unpopular among the Romans, who hated Cleopatra, and Caesar's grandnephew Octavian began plotting against the couple.

When Antony and Cleopatra's forces were defeated at the Battle of Actium in 31 B.C., they escaped to Egypt. A distraught Antony committed suicide by falling on his sword. Failing to seduce Octavian after he returned to Alexandria in 30 B.C., Cleopatra put an asp (snake) to her breast and its bite killed her. (The snake was sacred to the Egyptian sun god Ra.) Ptolemy XIV was later murdered, and Egypt became a province of Rome (a region controlled by the ancient Roman government).

33 B.C. ▪ Wang Zhaojung inspired writings

Wang Zhaojung was a beautiful consort (coruler) of the Chinese emperor Yuandi. When Zhaojung sat for her portrait, the court painter portrayed her as being ugly. Nevertheless she did not bribe him to change his depiction of her. On the basis of the unflattering portrait the emperor gave Zhaojung away as a bride to a chief of the Xiongnu, a powerful nomadic people (people who move from place to place within a given territory) in northern China. As Zhaojung was leaving the court the emperor saw her true beauty and realized he had made a mistake. It was too late, however, because he could not go back on his promise for fear of enraging the Xiongnu. The story of Wang Zhaojung has been the subject of numerous poems and plays.

c. 7 b.c. ▪ Mary gave birth to Jesus

Mary of Nazareth (a town in northern Israel) was the daughter of Anne (later St. Anne) and Joachim (later St. Joachim). Mary was descended from King David, one of the most important figures in the Hebrew religion. According to legend, Anne was freed from her barrenness (inability to have children) by an angel, who told her Mary would be born. Anne then dedicated her future child to the service of God. Mary grew up in Nazareth and became engaged to Joseph, a carpenter, who was also a descendant of David. According to the Gospel of Luke in the New Testament of the Bible, before Mary married Joseph, an angel of God named Gabriel appeared to her. Gabriel proclaimed that, although Mary was not married and remained a virgin, she would conceive a child by the Holy Spirit and give birth to God's son. (Gabriel's appearance has since been called the Annunciation.)

In the nearby town of Bethlehem, Mary had a son whom she named Jesus. (Some historians claim that she also had four other sons and at least two daughters after her marriage to Joseph.) Jesus became a Jewish rabbi, teaching a new form of religion, and was regarded as the "son of God" by his followers. In A.D. 30 Roman authorities who occupied Israel at that time arrested Jesus on charges of blasphemy (claiming to be a god) and sentenced him to death. Mary was present at the crucifixion of Jesus, who was later known as Christ the Savior by founders of the Christian religion. Mary was officially declared the Mother of God by a council at Ephesus, the seat of the Christian church in Byzantium (present-day Turkey), in A.D.

432. By the early twelfth century Mary had become the center of the Cult of the Virgin, particularly among Roman Catholics.

A.D. 19 ▪ Agrippina the Elder sought revenge

Agrippina the Elder (c. 14 B.C.–A.D. 33) was the grand-daughter of the Roman emperor Augustus and the daughter of Agrippa and his wife, Julia. She was married to Germanicus Caesar, a nephew of Augustus. Revered as a virtuous Roman matron, she had borne nine children by the age of twenty-nine. Her last child, Agrippina the Younger, would become the mother of the notorious ruler Nero.

In A.D. 19 Germanicus died. Suspecting that Emperor Tiberius had poisoned her husband, Agrippina began to plot revenge. The ambitious politician Sejanus, who himself wanted to overthrow the emperor, informed Tiberius that Agrippina was trying to get rid of him. In A.D. 29 Tiberius had Agrippina and her family exiled to Pandateria Island in the Bay of Naples, where she died on a hunger strike four years later. In A.D. 37 her son Gaius Caesar Germanicus became the Emperor Caligula, who was known for his mental instability. (*Also see entry dated A.D. 37: Agrippina the Younger began political scheming.*)

A.D. 37 ▪ Drusilla married Caligula

Drusilla was one of nine children of Agrippina the Elder and Germanicus Caesar. In A.D. 37 her brother Gaius Caesar Germanicus, called Caligula (because of the *caligae,* or sol-dier's boots, he wore), succeeded the Emperor Tiberius. When Caligula's wife died he became obsessed with Drusilla, forcing her to leave her husband and marry him. The Romans consid-ered marriage between brother and sister to be scandalous, but it was a common practice among Egyptian monarchs. In A.D. 39 Drusilla died suddenly. Caligula became totally unbalanced, declaring Drusilla a goddess and building a temple in her honor. He also proclaimed her birthday a holiday and ordered a statue of Venus, carved in Drusilla's likeness, to be placed in the forum (the marketplace, courts, and business center of an ancient Roman city). (*Also see entry dated A.D. 19: Agrippina the Elder sought revenge; and A.D. 37: Agrippina the Younger began political scheming.*)

A.D. 37 ▪ Agrippina the Younger began political scheming

Agrippina the Younger was the daughter of Agrippina the Elder and Germanicus Caesar. In A.D. 37, while married to Cneius Domitius Ahenobarbus, she gave birth to a son, Lucius Domitius Nero, who would be called Nero. That same year her brother Gaius Caesar Germanicus became the new emperor and took the name Caligula. Horrified by Caligula's excessive behavior as a ruler, Agrippina began conspiring against him. She was exiled by Caligula in A.D. 39 for improper sexual relations with a horse dealer, but she returned to Rome two years later when Caligula was murdered.

Shortly thereafter, Agrippina persuaded the wealthy Passienus Crispus to divorce his wife and marry her. (Agrippina's first husband, Ahenobarbus, died in A.D. 40.) Agrippina was soon widowed again, inheriting all of Crispus's property. She then turned her attention to her uncle, the Emperor Claudius I, whom she married and who adopted her son Nero. Agrippina dominated Claudius, convincing him to give Nero more power than his own son, Tiberius Claudius Britannicus. Nero ascended the throne when Claudius, reportedly poisoned at Agrippina's direction, died in A.D. 54. Agrippina continued to weave her political plots, but she eventually exhausted the patience of her son, who himself had become a dissolute ruler (one who lacks restraint or morals). At the urging of his mistress, Poppaea, Nero had Agrippina assassinated in A.D. 59.

A.D. 39 ▪ Sisters Trung Trac and Trung Nhi led revolt

Trung Trac was a wealthy widow living in Vietnam during Chinese domination of the country. Her husband had been killed by the Chinese and she herself had been raped. In retaliation she and her sister, Trung Nhi, raised an army of vassals (tenants of a feudal lord's estate) and led a rebellion. It was the first revolt against the Chinese in Southeast Asia. In their army was a woman warrior named Phung Thi Chinh, who was nine months pregnant. She is said to have stopped fighting only long enough to give birth and strap her baby on her back before rejoining the battle. The Trung sisters eventually committed suicide.

A.D. 38 ▪ Valeria Messalina paid for extravagance

When Valeria Messalina (A.D. 22–48) was sixteen, she married the then-fifty-year-old Claudius, who became emperor upon the death of his nephew Caligula. Before Claudius took the throne he had been considered slow-witted and incapable of performing the simplest public duties. Although he ruled better than anyone had expected, he was under the total control of Messalina and the empire's freedmen (men who had been freed from slavery). For seven years Messalina sold her influence to foreign allies (nations associated with each other by agreement) and indulged in displays of wealth that violated Roman laws against luxury. The common people hated her, blaming her for all of Rome's problems. In A.D. 48, while Claudius was out of the city, Messalina decided to marry one of her lovers, Gaius Silius. An angry Claudius ordered her execution, but she committed suicide with the assistance of a soldier. Informed of Messalina's death during a banquet, Claudius apparently did not even bother to interrupt dinner to inquire about the details. (*Also see entry dated A.D. 37: Agrippina the Younger began political scheming.*)

c. 40 ▪ Ban Zhao was born

Ban Zhao (c. A.D. 40–115) was the earliest known woman historian in China and perhaps the world. She wrote *Nu jie* ("Precepts for Women"), a guide to proper female behavior. With her father and her brother she also wrote the great *Han shu,* the definitive history of China.

50 ▪ Maria the Jewess established alchemy

Maria the Jewess probably lived and worked in Alexandria, Egypt. She was known by a number of names, including Maria Prophetissa and Miriam the Prophetus, with which she signed her scientific writings. Maria wrote extensively about her works, most notably an apparatus that she invented for distillation (a process that purifies a liquid). Resembling a modern-day double-boiler (a cooking utensil consisting of two pots, one on top of the other; boiling water in the lower pot is used to cook the contents of the upper pot), it was referred to as Maria's bath. (*Bain-marie,* the French term for double-boiler, has been traced to Maria's design.) She also invented an apparatus for processing metals; she believed that metals were living organisms, with either male or female gender.

53 ▪ Octavia doomed by marriage

Octavia (A.D. 37–62) was the daughter of Emperor Claudius I and Valeria Messalina. After Messalina was executed, Claudius married Agrippina the Younger. Agrippina's goal was to place her own son, Nero, on the throne. In A.D. 48 Agrippina engineered the downfall of Octavia's fiancé, Lucius Silanus, and arranged an engagement between the sixteen-year-old Octavia and Nero. Octavia married Nero in A.D. 53, but within a few years he had taken as his mistress Poppaea Sabina, the wife of one of his close friends. Urged on by Poppaea, Nero arranged his mother's death in A.D. 59. Three years later he divorced and banished Octavia. In response, the Rome populace rioted, replacing statues of Poppaea with those of Octavia. When Octavia resisted Nero's order to commit suicide, he directed his soldiers to slit her veins and suffocate her. Octavia's severed head was sent to Poppaea, who then married Nero. (*Also see entry dated A.D. 37: Agrippina the Younger began political scheming; and A.D. 38: Valeria Messalina paid for extravagance.*)

60 ▪ Boudicca led revolt

Boudicca was the wife of Prasutagus, king of the Icenians (a Celtic tribe that occupied modern-day England). At that time the Romans were disarming tribes in Britain and colonizing the area with Roman settlers. When Prasutagus died in A.D. 59 or 60, Boudicca took command and led a revolt against the

Romans. Within a year her rebel forces numbered over 120,000. They leveled several Roman villages, killing soldiers and civilians alike. By A.D. 61 the Romans regained control as the cavalry (soldiers on horseback) handily defeated the poorly armed Icenian troops. It is believed that Boudicca escaped and then poisoned herself.

98 ▪ Germanic tribes worshiped Nerthus

The goddess Nerthus (Mother Earth) was celebrated in a ritual procession described by the Roman writer Tacitus in *Germania* (A.D. 98). It was the first known written account of Germanic religious rites. During the procession all fighting ceased, weapons and iron tools were laid aside, and doors were opened in hospitality. Nerthus was one of the many aspects of Freya, the Great Goddess of northern Europe who ruled the heavens before Odin (Woden), the supreme god and creator, arrived from the East. Indeed, Nerthus is believed to have taught Odin everything he knew about magic and divine power.

c. 100 ▪ Himiko and Jingu ruled as shamanesses

Shinto, the original religion of Japan, is based on the view of the world in which *kami* (divine spirits) interact with humans in both positive and negative ways. Since ancient times some women have fulfilled the role of shamaness—a person having supernatural powers who is able to communicate with and interpret the way of the *kami*. Japan's early empresses, the legendary Himiko (reigned from 180 to 248) and Jingu (reigned late fourth to early fifth centuries) practiced shamanism. At times, shamanesses would go into trances and, when in a state of possession, make predictions of future events or give advice to their followers.

100 ▪ Beruyah was authority on Talmud

During the first century A.D., Beruyah was an influential authority on the Talmud, a collection of interpretations and explanations by scholars of the Oral Law of the Judaic religion. (The Oral Law is distinct from the Written Law, called the Torah.) During Beruyah's time the Talmud consisted of the Mishna, which was compiled by *tannaim* (Jewish sages). The Talmud continues to be the accepted authority by Orthodox Jews (those who observe original Hebrew teachings), and twentieth-century scholars still respect the opinions of Beruyah.

Roman Women Were Gladiators

In the mid-second century women gladiators, or gladiatrices, entertained Roman spectators by fighting to the death in public and private combats. Eventually women were banned from fighting in companies against each other or individually against dwarfs.

190 ▪ Empress Pimiku built Shrine of Ise

Pimiku (?-247), the first known ruler of Japan, reigned until her death. Although she was never married, in 234 she had a daughter. Pimiku is credited with building the Shrine of Ise, the most important shrine of the Shinto religion in Japan. (Founded in Japan, Shinto is devoted to the worship of nature gods and regards the empress as a descendant of the sun goddess.)

203 ▪ Perpetua martyred by Romans

Perpetua (?–203), the daughter of Vibia Perpetua, was born in Carthage, North Africa. During the reign of the Roman emperor Septimus Severus, Perpetua was thrown into prison for being a Christian. Her slave, Felicitas, and three male Christians accompanied her. As she awaited death in the amphitheater (Christians were tortured and killed in large public arenas), Perpetua wrote part of the *Passion of St. Perpetua and Felicity,* a valuable account of the experiences of early Christian martyrs (people who die for a religious cause). In the early nineteenth century a church was built in honor of Perpetua and Felicitas on the site of their burial.

248 ▪ Trieu Au lead army against the Chinese

Trieu Au (222–248) was a Vietnamese resistance leader who organized an army of 1,000 troops to drive out the Chinese, who occupied Vietnam. Artists' drawings show her wearing golden armor and holding a sword in each hand as she rides into battle on an elephant. Although Trieu Au's brother begged her to change her mind, she reportedly said, "I want to rail against wind and tide, kill the whales in the ocean, sweep the whole country to save people from slavery, and I have no desire to take abuse." Within six months Trieu Au and her army were defeated. Determined not to surrender, she took her own life. A temple was built in Trieu Au's honor and stands today in Vietnam.

c. 251 ▪ Taoist leader Wei Huacun was born

Wei Huacun (c. A.D. 251–334), an important Chinese Taoist (see definition below) leader, was highly educated, and although she was married she lived apart from her husband. Taoist divinities are said to have revealed sacred texts to her, which she then transmitted to the human world. This pattern of communication, by which male divinities transmit texts to male humans through a female intermediary, remains common in Taoism. (Taoism is a mystical Chinese religion that stresses "the way"—living a life of simplicity and harmony with nature to ensure order, good fortune , and long life.)

267 ▪ Zenobia extended power of Palmyra

Zenobia, who was of Arab descent, was the wife of King Odaenathus of Palmyra (an ancient city in Syria). When Odaenathus was murdered in A.D. 267—some accounts suggest Zenobia was involved in his death—she took the throne as regent (substitute ruler) for her son Wahballat. She immediately set out to extend the power of Palmyra into the Roman empire, commanding military campaigns that resulted in the annexation (addition; taking over) of most of Syria and parts of Egypt. Zenobia's ambition was thwarted in A.D. 272, however, when she declared her son emperor of the new territories. The Roman emperor Aurelian seized Palmyra, captured Zenobia, and took her to Rome. After A.D. 274 she lived in retirement in Tibur (now Tivoli, Italy). Although Zenobia was admired for her beauty and intelligence, her name has become synonymous with ruthlessness.

310 ▪ St. Catherine executed for conversion

Catherine (290-310) was born into a royal family in Alexandria, Egypt. At the age of 18, after she had converted to

Women Embark on Religious Pilgrimages

Pilgrimages (journeys, usually by foot) to religious shrines throughout Europe and to the Holy Land (present-day Israel) became fashionable in the fourth century. Women of all ranks participated. In order to take part in a pilgrimage both men and women were required to walk at least sixty miles and to carry a certificate from a bishop or priest proving they were true pilgrims. They also carried a staff (long walking stick) and a scrip (pouch decorated with an emblem). Pilgrim routes developed between Britain and the Holy Land (Israel), passing through Rome, Italy. Rest stations such as the Hospital of the Pellegrini in Rome accommodated as many as seven thousand weary travelers.

Christianity, she denounced Emperor Maxentius for persecuting Christians. Attempting to silence Catherine, the emperor forced her to have a discussion about religion with 50 pagan (non-Christian) philosophers. When the philosophers found no flaws in her argument, Maxentius had them executed. Then, learning that Catherine had converted his own wife and several soldiers to Christianity, Maxentius ordered Catherine to be bound to a spiked wheel—later known as a "Catherine wheel"—and her body broken. The wheel broke instead, so Catherine was beheaded. Her body was taken to Mount Sinai, a holy Christian site on the Sinai Peninsula in northeast Egypt, where a shrine is now on display in St. Catherine's monastery. Because of the manner of her martyrdom (dying for a religious cause) Catherine is depicted in religious pictures carrying a wheel.

324 ▪ Helena founded Christian churches

Helena (c. 250–330), mother of the Roman emperor Constantine the Great, is also considered to have been the mother of Christianity. A devout Christian, she made a pilgrimage in 324 to Jerusalem, where she found pieces of wood she claimed were remnants of the cross on which Jesus Christ had been crucified. As a result of this experience, she founded the Church of the Holy Sepulchre in Jerusalem and the Church of the Nativity in Nazareth (on the site where she believed Jesus was born). She established many other churches during her lifetime, and upon her death she was buried in Constantinople (now Istanbul, Turkey). Around 850, however, her body was moved to the Abbey of Hautvillers near Rheims, France. In the Eastern Orthodox church, her feast day is celebrated on May 21.

c. 370 ▪ Su Hui created poems and word puzzles

The skilled Chinese poet and weaver Su Hui invented the palindrome (verses that reads the same backward and forward). Her palindrome featured Chinese characters woven in brocade in a square, 29 characters by 29 characters. The poems embedded in the fabric could be read from top to bottom, from right to left, or from left to right. As many as four thousand poems have been found in Sui Hui's palindrome. At that time in China, weaving was regarded as "women's work"; so Su Hui managed to express her literary skills while doing so-called "women's work."

370 ▪ Hypatia of Alexandria was born

Hypatia (c. 370–415) was born in Alexandria, Egypt. As a child she was taught mathematics by her father, the noted mathematician Theon. She also studied in Athens, Greece, with the author Plutarch the Younger and his daughter Asclepegeneia. Described by ancient writers as being both beautiful and intelligent, Hypatia surpassed her contemporaries with her knowledge of a variety of subjects. Apparently she was never married. Her lectures on Greek philosophers Plato and Aristotle, which she conducted in the center of Alexandria, were attended by students, public officials, and fellow scholars. She is said to have dressed in a tattered cloak, imitating the ancient philosophers during her talks.

One of Hypatia's students was Synesius of Cyrene, who became bishop of Ptolemais. Seven letters from Synesius to Hypatia have survived throughout the years, and they reveal the extent of Hypatia's scientific work. In 415 Hypatia was accused of having incited a confrontation (the confrontation actually occurred three years earlier) between Christian monks and a public official, at which time a monk was killed. At the direction of Archbishop Cyril of Alexandria, monks pulled Hypatia from her chariot and dragged her into the cathedral. Stripping her naked and killing her, they reportedly cut her body into pieces and burned it.

390 ▪ Queen Prabhāvata Gupta introduced Gupta culture

Prabhāvata Gupta began her 20-year reign of the Vākāta kingdom in the Deccan region of southern India when her husband, King Rudrasena II, died in 390. Prabhāvata has been credited with introducing her native Gupta culture to the Vākāta. At the height of the Gupta empire (c. 320–c. 550), which encompassed most of northern India, the Gupta dynasty (a succession of rulers from the same family) promoted painting, sculpture, philosophy, and mathematics.

Matches Invented by Chinese Women

Women from the Ch'i province of northern China have been credited with inventing matches in A.D. 577. The invention resulted from their need for a more convenient way to start fires for cooking and heating.

c. 391–408 ▪ St. Olympias ordained as Christian minister

At the age of eighteen St. Olympias (366–408) married the prefect (chief official) of the city of Constantinople (now Istanbul, Turkey). After her husband's death two years later, she refused to marry again, even though her great wealth and personal charm attracted a variety of men. Instead, Olympias began giving her money to charities. In 391 she was ordained a minister of the Christian church.

Olympias was a strong supporter and friend of the archbishop of Constantinople, St. John Chrysostom, an outspoken reformer who made many enemies with his attacks on church corruption. In 403 Chrysostom was expelled as a bishop by the Empress Eudoxia and a year later banished from Constantinople. In protest, Olympias organized an attempt to burn down the cathedral. When arrested, she spoke out boldly to the authorities in support of Chrysostom and refused to recognize his successor as archbishop, an act for which she was heavily fined. Although she risked arrest, endured continued persecutions, and was driven from place to place for the rest of her life, Olympias stood by Chrysostom until his death in 407.

400 ▪ Hua Mu-Lan took her father's place in battle

Hua Mu-Lan was the most famous of many Chinese women warriors. According to legend, after winning a sword fight with her father she disguised herself as a man and took his place in battle for 12 years. Mu-Lan's commanding officer was so impressed with her bearing and performance that he offered his daughter to her in marriage. Numerous plays and poems have been based on Hua Mu-Lan's story.

c. 451 ▪ St. Geneviève turned back Atilla the Hun

St. Geneviève (420–500), the legendary patron saint of Paris, France, is credited with saving the city from Atilla, king of the Huns (warlike people from north-central Asia). When she was fifteen years old Geneviève took vows and received her veil as a dedicated virgin. After the Huns had invaded France and Atilla was advancing toward Paris, Geneviève told people not to abandon their homes. Although filled with fear, they heeded her advice and watched as Atilla turned away and instead attacked the nearby city of Orléans.

Believing Geneviève's prayers had protected them, the Parisians regarded her as a prophet and a holy woman. Later the people followed her in a convoy up the River Seine to Tropes to bring back supplies when the Franks (Germanic tribes from along the Rhine River) blockaded Paris. Geneviève was also able to persuade the Frankish leader Childeric to accept her pleas on behalf of prisoners of war. Near the end of her life she convinced King Clovis of the Franks to release some prisoners and to save others from severe punishment. The people of Paris continued to look to Geneviève as their protector even after her death. In 1129 an epidemic of ergot (fungus) poisoning came to an end when her relics were carried in a public procession, an event that is still celebrated each year in the churches of Paris. St. Geneviève's feast day is celebrated on January 3.

c. 480 ▪ St. Brigid founded convent

St. Brigid (c. 450–523) is one of the patron saints of Ireland, honored as highly as her co-patron, St. Patrick, who is credited with introducing Christianity to Ireland. She founded the first women's religious community at Kildare, the site of a popular shrine to the goddess Bridgit before the Christianization of Ireland. Brigid may never have existed as a person but may instead be a Christian embodiment (or representation) of the Celtic triune (consisting of three parts) moon goddess Bridgit. St. Brigid's Feast Day—February 1—is the same day as the goddess Bridgit's feast, and fires were lit for both celebrations. St. Brigid's nuns allegedly tended a sacred fire that men were not allowed to approach; many priestesses in goddess temples watched over similar fires.

c. 496 ▪ Clotild converted king

Clotild, alternately spelled Clotilda or Clotilde (c. 475–545), was born into the royal family of Burgundy (a region in present-day France) around 475. When she was about eighteen years old she married Clovis, king of the Franks (Germanic tribes from along the Rhine River who settled in present-day France). They had four sons. Around the year 496 Clotild was influential in converting Clovis to Christianity. The conversion of the king had important consequences for the future of France because the Franks became allied with the Roman Catholic church. After her husband's death in 511, Queen Clotild devoted herself to religious pursuits, becoming famous for her devotion to God and her generosity to the church. Clotild died in 545 and was named a saint.

c. 500 ▪ Devi became supreme deity

Devi, whose name means "goddess," is the supreme deity of the Hindu religion. Without her, it is believed that no other god or goddess has form or power. Therefore, all the gods and goddesses worshiped by the Hindu people are connected to Devi, the source of all being. The earliest known text that speaks of the goddess as the supreme deity dates from around 500.

c. 526—535 ▪ Amalasuntha helped Gothic society

Amalasuntha (498–535) was the daughter of Theodoric the Great, Ostrogothic king of Italy. (The Ostrogoths were the eastern division of the Goths, a Germanic people.) Upon her father's death in 526, Amalasuntha became regent (substitute ruler) for her son Athalaric. When Athalaric died in 534, she and her husband, Theodahad, became joint rulers of Italy. The following year Amalasuntha was deposed by Gothic nobles who did not approve of her friendly relations with the Byzantine emperor Justinian I. Shortly thereafter the queen was strangled in her bath while being held prisoner. Having a deep appreciation of ancient Roman culture, Amalasuntha had tried to improve Gothic society by encouraging literacy and learning. However, she was unable to make changes in Gothic Italy during the nine years she held power.

Law Restricts Inheritance of Land

The Salians, Germanic Franks living in Gaul (present-day France, Holland, and Belgium), issued a code of laws that prohibited women from inheriting land. Later in the sixth century the so-called Salic Law was revised to allow a daughter to inherit land if her father had no male heirs. Nonetheless, the French for centuries cited the Salic Law as the authority for denying the crown of France to a woman.

c. 527 ▪ Theodora was influential ruler

Theodora (497–548) rose from obscure origins to become a powerful empress in the Byzantine empire. She was the daughter of a bear keeper at the circus in Constantinople (now Istanbul, Turkey). After a career as an actress or circus performer and possibly a courtesan (prostitute), Theodora attracted the attention of Justinian, a court official whom she married around 525. Two years later when he became Emperor Justinian I, he appointed Theodora joint ruler of the Byzantine empire.

For over twenty years, until her death in 548, Theodora took an active role in governing the region. According to a famous story, Justinian was ready to flee for his life during the Nika (victory) rebellion against his economic and religious policies in 532. At the urging of Theodora, however, he remained in Constantinople and saved the throne. Theodora also influenced Justinian's policies toward the Monophysites, a Christian sect that believed Jesus Christ possessed only a divine (or heavenly) nature. Inspired by Theodora's Christian faith, Justinian persuaded the Monophysites to accept the view that Christ was both human and divine. Theodora is depicted in mosaics (pictures made of small pieces of tile) in the church of San Vitale in Ravenna, Italy.

c. 562 ▪ Fredegunde caused assassination

Fredegunde (?–597) was originally a servant in the household of Chilperic I, king of Neutrisia, a region in the northwestern area of the kingdom of the Franks (present-day France). She became his mistress, then married him after engineering the murder of his previous wife, Galeswintha, in 562. The murder began Fredegunde's disastrous feud with Galeswintha's sister, Queen Brunhilda of Austrasia (parts of modern-day France and Bavaria) in the eastern Frankish kingdom. The feud led to a half-century of warfare between Neutrisia and Austrasia. Fredegunde was also responsible for the deaths of Brunhilda's husband, Sigebert I, as well as her own stepchildren. After Chilperic was murdered in 584, she became regent (substitute ruler) for her son Clotaire II. Fredegunde died around the year 597 and is remembered as reckless, ruth-less, and cruel. (*Also see entry dated c. 567: Brunhilda conducted bloody warfare.*)

c. 567 ▪ Brunhilda conducted bloody warfare

Brunhilda was the daughter of Athanagild, a Visigothic (of Germanic origin) king in Spain, and wife of King Sigebert of Austrasia (part of present-day France and Bavaria). In 562 Fredegunde, wife of King Chilperic I of Neutrisia, instigated the murder of Brunhilda's sister Galeswintha. Seeking revenge, Brunhilda plunged the kingdom into fifty years of bloody and vicious warfare. The struggle between Austrasia and Neutrisia continued through the death of Sigebert in 575 and the murder of Chilperic in 584. Throughout the reigns of her son Childebert II and her two grandsons, Brunhilda was the actual ruler of Austrasia. In 592 she annexed Burgundy into Austrasia. Although Brunhilda was known for her political skills, she was hated by the Frankish noblemen under her control. Finally they betrayed her to Fredegunde's son, Clortair II, who had her put to death in 613, when she was eighty years old. (*Also see entry dated c. 562: Fredegunde caused assassination.*)

592 ▪ Suiko became Japanese sovereign

Empress Suiko (554–626) ascended to the throne through the assistance of her mother's family, the powerful Soga, thus becoming the first woman sovereign (supreme ruler) of Japan. She was mainly a shamaness (priestess), who prepared meals to offer the ancestral Shinto deities. (Shintoism, the national religion of Japan, involved the worship of nature gods and recognized the emperor as a descendant of the sun goddess Amaterasu o Mikami.) Suiko reigned at a time of conflict between two opposing factions, or groups: conservatives who championed the Shinto religion, and other ruling families, like the Soga, who promoted Buddhism. Buddhism was founded in India in 525 B.C. by Siddhartha Gautama, known as the Buddha. According to his teachings, life consists of suffering that can be relieved only through mental and moral self-purification. Suiko resolved the conflicts in these two religions by continu-

Muhammad Replaces Female-Centered Religion With Islam

The three goddesses Al-Uzza, Al-Lat, and Menat (or Manat) were the supreme religious trinity of pre-Islamic Arabia, where they were worshiped for centuries. They were three distinct aspects of the same goddess: Al-Uzza was the young warrior; Al-Lat the fertile mother; and Menat the aged bestower of fate and death. Muhammad, the founder of Islam, worshiped the triune (consisting of three parts) goddess before overthrowing this female-centered religion and replacing it with the male-centered religion of Islam in 622.

ing to serve the Shinto deities and also supporting Buddhism. Her reign was a golden period for the establishment of Buddhist temples and the creation of Buddhist-inspired art.

594 ▪ Khadija married Muhammad

Khadija (c. 564–619) was a wealthy Arab widow who hired Muhammad (sometimes spelled Mohammed or Mahomet; c. 570–632) to escort a camel caravan to Syria around the turn of the seventh century. Upon his return they were married and Muhammad became a merchant. Because Khadija was wealthy, Muhammad had considerable free time to meditate. He reportedly spent several years in a cave where he had religious visions. Khadija encouraged his religious ideas, which he wrote in the Koran and which attracted many followers. Khadija was Muhammad's first disciple. She died in 619. During their marriage they had a daughter, Fatima.

The Koran became the basis for the Islamic religion and law of the Muslims, who are now a major percentage of the world population. According to the Muslims, Allah is the only true god and Muhammad was his prophet. (*Also see entry dated 606: Birth of Fatima.*)

606 ▪ Birth of Fatima

Fatima (606–632) was the daughter of the Muslim prophet Muhammad and his first wife, Khadija. She married the caliph (successor of Muhammad and head of Islam) Ali, with whom she had three sons. Two of their sons, Hassan and Hussein, founded the Fatimid dynasty that ruled Egypt and North Africa from 909 to 1171. Now revered by all branches of Islam, she became the subject of numerous mysteries and legends. (*Also see entry dated 594: Khadija married Muhammad.*)

610 ▪ Baudonivia wrote early biography

Baudonivia, a Frankish nun who lived at the convent established by Queen Radegunda at Poitiers, completed a book titled *The Life of St. Radegund*. Writing some twenty years after the former queen's death, Baudonivia relied on information she obtained mainly from people who knew her subject.

c. 614 ▪ Birth of Hilda, abbess of Whitby

Hilda (c. 614–680), abbess (a woman who heads a convent) of Whitby, played an active role in establishing Christianity in England. As a great-niece of the king of Northumbria (an Anglo-Saxon kingdom in Britain), Hilda belonged to Anglo-Saxon royalty. She was baptized at the age of thirteen but did not become a nun until she was thirty-three. Thereafter Hilda served as abbess of several English religious houses, the most famous being the double monastery at Whitby, a Roman Catholic institution for both men and women. She had the authority of a bishop, although she could not preside at communion or administer other sacraments. Hilda was an able and devout administrator, as witnessed by the fact that five monks of Whitby became bishops. She was also influential at the Synod of Whitby in 664, where Irish and Roman Catholic clergy settled their differences over rituals and ensured the unity of Christianity in the British Isles.

c. 630 ▪ Birth of Japanese poet Nukata no Okimi

Nukata (Nukada) no Okimi (c. 630–690) was the most outstanding Japanese woman poet of her generation. Her mother's family had a rich tradition of storytelling. Influenced by this background, Nukata distinguished herself at the imperial court for her literary skill. She was a Shinto priestess and an imperial consort (wife of an emperor). In one of her most famous poems she argues that autumn is aesthetically (in beauty) and emotionally more satisfying than spring. Twelve of her poems are compiled in the *Manyoshu* (c. 759), the earliest extant collection of Japanese poetry.

c. 632 ▪ Sonduk built first observatory in Far East

Sonduk was born in Korea. Because there were no males from the Silla dynasty (a succession of rulers from the same family) to take the throne, she became queen in 632 and ruled for 15 years. According to legend, at age seven she had explained to her father why the peony (a fragrant flower) should have no scent. Upon discovering that she was correct, the king reportedly replied, "My wise little daughter! She shall reign when I am gone." During her reign Sonduk built Ch'omsong-dae (Tower of the Moon and Stars), the first known observatory (a building equipped for astronomers) in the Far East (the countries of eastern and southeastern Asia). The Ch'omsong-dae remained standing through the twentieth century.

c. 657 ▪ St. Balthild rose from slavery

Balthild (also Bathild or Baldhild) was an English girl who was captured and forced to be a slave for Erchinoald, mayor of the palace of King Clovis II of the Frankish kingdom (present-day France). Eventually she attracted the notice of the king, who married her sometime around the year 648. The couple had three sons—Clothar III, Theuderic III, and Childeric II—and when Clovis died in 657 Balthild became queen regent (substitute ruler) for her son Clothar. As queen regent, she opposed the slave trade and encouraged religious vocations, giving many gifts to monasteries and founding convents at Chelles and Corbie. When her regency (period of rule) ended in 664, ambitious nobles forced her to leave the court and retire to the convent at Chelles, where she lived as a nun until her death in 680. Her feast day is celebrated on January 30.

681 ▪ Empress Gemmei ordered history text

Empress Gemmei (661–721) ascended to the throne of Japan in 707. During her reign the new capital in Nara was completed, and it became an important Japanese political and cultural center. Gemmei also oversaw the first attempt to replace the barter system (paying for goods with other goods) with the use of copper coins. However, her most significant contribution was the decree that the *Kojiki* ("Chronicle of Ancient Things") be written from the transcription of orally transmitted tales. Recording the rise of the imperial clan (ruling family) and other aristocratic families in Japan from the beginning of the universe to the reign of Empress Suiko (ruled from 592 to 628), the three-volume work was completed in 712.

690 ▪ Wu Ze–tian was female emperor of China

Wu Ze-tian (624–705) was initially in the harem (group of wives) of Emperor Tai Zong of the Tang dynasty. When the emperor died in 649, his son, Gao Zong, adopted Wu Ze-tian into his own harem and had a daughter with her. The ruthless Wu Ze-tian became Gao Zong's empress by strangling her own daughter and then blaming it on the ruling empress, Wang. When Gao Zong later became physically frail, Wu Ze-tian took over state affairs and began formulating new policies that appealed to a wide variety of social groups. In 690 Wu Ze-tian proclaimed herself emperor and renamed herself Wu Zhou to signify the end of the Tang dynasty. Age and corruption led to her being deposed, or removed from her position, in 705. Wu Ze-tian died later that year.

Japanese Ideals of Feminine Beauty

Japanese ideals of feminine beauty developed at the imperial court. Women's clothing ceased to imitate Chinese styles and became more characteristically Japanese. Women at court wore twelve layers of loosely fitting robes, each of a slightly greater length, in a slightly different shade. Women of the lower classes wore simpler clothes, including short, sleeveless robes. Their hair was ideally long (actually floor-length), glossy, and worn loosely. Cosmetics were an important part of the feminine ideal. Women shaved their eyebrows, replacing them with a thin painted line, and they wore white face powder and rouge. When girls reached puberty, they began to blacken their teeth.

c. 694 ▪ Empress Jito centralized Japanese state

Empress Jito (c. 645–703) concentrated the power of the Japanese state in a centralized system of government. Initially she helped her husband, Emperor Temmu, ascend to the throne by developing successful military strategies and commanding the troops stationed at Ise. (The Ise Shrine, dedicated to the sun goddess, symbolizes imperial rule, or rule of a kingdom by an emperor.) Jito educated herself on matters of law and drafted regulations during Temmu's reign (673–686). Following his death in 694 she took the throne and began to make significant changes in government. Among them were the creation of policy-making groups and the elimination of rule by various chieftains (meaning all power in the Japanese state was placed under a single sovereign or ruler).

c. 700 ▪ Poet Sano no Chigami born

Sano no Chigami was born in Japan around 700. She was a palace attendant of low rank who served the high priestess of the Shrine of Ise. In violation of a strict taboo against the presence of men in the palace of the priestess, she had a secret affair. When she and her lover were discovered, she was sent into exile (forced to leave Japan). Chigami wrote a series of sixty-three poems about her forbidden love that are included in the *Manyoshu,* the first great anthology of Japanese poetry, published in 759.

c. 700 ▪ Nieh Yin-niang, a Chinese "Robin Hood"

Chinese woman warrior Nieh Yin-niang is celebrated as a one-woman Robin Hood (a legendary sixteenth-century British hero who robbed from the rich and gave what he stole to the poor). Taught swordsmanship by a nun around 700, Nieh Yin-niang is said to have helped the weak and attacked criminals.

c. 710 ▪ Lioba helped Christianize Germany

Lioba (c. 710–782) was born in Wessex, England, of a noble family. Upon completion of her education in an Anglo-Saxon convent, she became a nun. Lioba was related to St. Boniface, the English monk who undertook the Christianization of the Germans. In 748 she followed Boniface to Germany, where she aided his missionary effort and became abbess, or head, of the Benedictine convent at Bischofsheim. Lioba was noted for her wisdom, devotion, and charity in this position for twenty-eight years. When she died around 782, she was buried near Boniface.

720 ▪ Empress Gensho ordered second national history

Japanese empress Gensho (680–748) succeeded her mother, Empress Gemmei, ascending to the throne in 715.

During Gensho's reign, centralized rule was extended farther into Japan with the Yoro Code, which was established in 718. Two years later Japan's second official national history, the *Nihongi* ("Chronicle of Japan"), was completed in accordance with Gensho's orders. (*Also see entry dated 681: Empress Gemmei ordered national history.*)

729 ▪ Komyo promoted Buddhism

Through the influence of her family (the powerful Fujiwara), Empress Komyo (701–760) became the first woman not of noble blood to serve as an imperial consort (coruler) in Japan. A devout Buddhist, she suggested that Emperor Shomu (reigned from 715 to 749) establish government-sponsored Buddhist temples and convents throughout Japan. Komyo sponsored charitable foundations that ministered to the poor and sick.

c. ▪ 755 Yang Guifei led emperor astray

Yang Guifei was a paradigm (example) of the "state-toppling beauty," a beautiful woman who poses a threat to a nation's political order. History tells us that Emperor Xuanzong became so infatuated with her that he appointed her corrupt male relatives to important positions and, even worse, neglected affairs of state. The result was the catastrophic rebellion of An Lushan in 755. Imperial troops were so certain that the root of the problem was Yang Guifei that they refused to fight to defend the throne unless the emperor had her executed. The emperor made his choice, and Yang Guifei met her death. The tragic story has been the subject of countless poems, plays, and stories.

797 ▪ Irene ruled alone

Irene the Athenian (c. 752–803) was born in Athens around 752. She was well educated and soon married the

Empress Irene conspired against her son Constantine VI in order to retain control of the Byzantine government.

Byzantine emperor Leo IV, becoming regent (substitute ruler) for their young son Constantine VI upon Leo's death in 780. Irene later conspired against her son in order to retain control of the government by having him blinded and possibly murdered in 797. For the next five years she controlled the empire alone, becoming the first woman in recorded European history to rule in her own name. Irene was instrumental in restoring the use of icons (religious images) in the Byzantine empire, a practice prohibited in the early eighth century. For this service to the Greek Orthodox church, she was named a saint. Nonetheless, her enemies succeeded in overthrowing her in 802, sending her into exile. Irene died later that year.

800 ▪ Composer Kassiane was born

Kassiane, also known as Elkasia Kassia (c. 800–c. 843; some sources give birth date as 810 and death date as 867), was born in Constantinople (present-day Istanbul, Turkey). She was the abbess (head administrator) of the Icassion convent, which she founded at Constantinople. Kassiane is best known, however, as the composer of 23 hymns for Eastern Orthodox church services. (The Eastern Orthodox church is a community of Christian churches located principally in the Middle East and Eastern Europe. It differs from the Roman Catholic church by not acknowledging the authority of the pope.) Kassiane's most famous hymn is "The Troparion of Kassiane."

819 ▪ Queen Judith married Louis the Pious

Judith was a member of the powerful Welf (Guelph) family who lived in a region of Europe that is now Germany. She became the second wife of Emperor Louis the Pious, the son of Charlemagne, who ruled from 814 to 840. Her influence on her husband's government aroused some resentment, and she endangered the kingdom by insisting that a portion of the realm be given to her son Charles the Bald (823–877) to rule. At an imperial meeting at Worms in 829, she finally succeeded in gaining parts of Swabia, Alsace, and Burgundy for Charles. When Louis's sons from his first marriage refused to accept this new division with their half-brother, they ignited a civil war that severely weakened the Carolingian empire. Judith died in 843, a few months before the empire was permanently divided into three parts. The eastern and western parts, which were separated by a middle realm of Lotharingia, became France and Germany.

c. 841 ▪ Dhuoda wrote court handbook

Dhuoda was a member of the higher nobility in the Carolingian empire (the Frankish kingdom enlarged by Charlemagne). She was married to Bernard, a duke involved in the secret schemes of the Carolingian courts. Her husband settled her in a small town in southern France, rarely visiting her, although they had two sons. Bernard took the elder son, William, age fourteen, from Dhuoda to live at the court of Charles the Bald, the monarch of the western third of the empire (present-day France). Dhuoda wrote a handbook for her son's use at court, emphasizing service to God and the ideals of noble existence. This small work gave remarkable insight into the life of a well-educated woman in the early medieval period, a time of great political unrest. Because Dhuoda mentioned in the book that she was seriously ill, she may have died shortly after finishing it in 843. (*Also see entry dated 819: Queen Judith married Louis the Pious*)

c. 857 ▪ Queen Theutberga resisted divorce

Theutberga was the wife of King Lothar II of Lotharingia, an area that covered the modern countries of Belgium, the Netherlands, Luxembourg, Switzerland, and parts of France and Germany. During his reign from 855 to 869, the couple had no children—and therefore no heirs to the throne. Meanwhile, Lothar wanted to marry his mistress, Waldrada, by whom he had a son who could inherit his kingdom. In 857 Lothar accused his wife of adultery so he could gain a divorce. Theutberga, however, protested her husband's false accusations. Although the clergy in Lothar's kingdom agreed to the king's divorce, Pope Nicholas I (head of the Roman Catholic church from 858 to 867) prohibited the action. The pope's intervention signaled an increasing control by the papacy (church government) on the laws of marriage. The dynasty thus ended with Lothar's death, while both Waldrada and Theutberga retired to monasteries. The Lotharingian middle realm was then destroyed by various competitors, and its remnants were fought over by France and Germany for the next thousand years.

877 ▪ Birth of Lady Ise

The Japanese court lady known as Lady Ise (877–940) was considered one of the most accomplished poets of her time. Her verses contain both wit and great passion, and more than five hundred have been compiled in various anthologies.

c. 90 ▪ Calligrapher Lady Li Fu-jen was born

Lady Li Fu-jen (c. 907–960) was born in China and worked as a calligrapher (a person who copies documents in elaborate writing). She is credited with originating bamboo painting, a technique that involves using a sharpened bamboo stick to create a painting.

911 ▪ Aethelflaed began ruling Mercia

Aethelflaed (Ethelfleda) was the daughter of Alfred the Great, king of the West-Saxons in an area that is now part of England. Sometime around 880 Alfred gave Aethelflaed in marriage to Aethelred, earl of the West Mercians, who inhabited present-day central England. The marriage was part of Alfred's plan to create a unified England. Following Alfred's death in 899, Aethelflaed's brother Edward was crowned king of Wessex and continued his father's policies. Aethelflaed and Aethelred, apparently acting with equal authority, defended Mercia against invading Danes, Northmen, and Welshmen. Mercia and Wessex cooperated in erecting fortresses to ward off Viking raids.

The poor health of Aethelflaed's husband forced her to act as regent (substitute ruler). After his death in 911, "The Lady of the Mercians," as Aethelflaed was now called, ruled

Ritual Sacrifice of Women

Ibn Fadhlan, an Arabian traveler and writer, witnessed the burial of a man, presumably a prominent Norse trader, along the Volga River in what is now Russia. He wrote a detailed account of the ritual, in which a slave girl was drugged, killed, and cremated along with the deceased to serve as his companion in death. Such sacrifices of women at the burials of their husbands or masters occurred in eastern Europe during the early medieval period (500–900). There are also several reports among Slavic (eastern European) populations of the voluntary self-cremation of widows, known as *sati*, at the funeral pyres of their husbands. *Sati* suggests that women were completely subjugated to (or under the control of) men at the time. The practice ended in Europe with the coming of Christianity, but it survived until modern times in parts of India.

Mercia alone for seven years. She led troops into combat, increased the extent of the territory under her control, and built a number of fortresses throughout the land. Aethelflaed's efforts led in 918 to the eventual defeat of the Vikings (pirate invaders from a region in present-day Scandinavia) six months after her death. She is also credited with bringing about the political unification of England.

c. 935 ▪ Birth of Hrosvitha

Hrosvitha (also Hrotsvit or Roswitha) (c. 935–1000) was born into the royal Saxon family. As a child she entered the wealthy, independent nunnery of Gandersheim. Hrosvitha gained a fine education, perhaps at the royal court, and became a canoness (a woman who lived in a religious community but was not a nun). She wrote books about saints' lives and compiled histories of the royal family and of her monastery. Most importantly, Hrosvitha was a dramatist, writing some of the first plays since antiquity (the ancient Greek and Roman period). Drawing on the works of classical writers (especially the Roman playwright Terence), she adapted their themes and transformed them into stories about Christian saints and martyrs. She also wrote narrative poems based on Christian legends. Hrosvitha is considered the first known German woman poet.

c. 945 ▪ Princess Olga became Russian ruler

Olga was born in the principality of Kiev, a region that eventually became part of western Russia (the present-day Republic of Ukraine). When her husband, Prince Igor I, was assassinated in 945, Princess Olga served as regent (substitute ruler) for her son until 964, thus becoming the first female ruler in recorded Russian history. During her reign Olga expanded the borders of Kiev and converted to Christianity. She was probably baptized into the Orthodox church in Constantinople (now Istanbul, Turkey) in 957. Her efforts to bring Christianity to Russia were fulfilled three decades later by her grandson, Prince Vladimir. For her service to the faith Olga was named the first Russian saint of the Orthodox church.

c. 950 ▪ Japanese court lady wrote classic diary

Kagero Nikki ("The Gossamer Years") is a classic of Japanese confessional literature that depicts a court lady's unhappiness in her marriage. The name of the author is not known, since she referred to herself only as the wife of Fujiwara Kaneie (928–990) or the mother of Fujiwara Michitsuna (955–1020). She was a secondary wife in a system of polygamy, wherein a man had several wives. Her position was therefore uncertain, and she recorded in her diary her feelings of betrayal and rejection. While her son brought her satisfaction, her marriage caused her only frustration and bitterness. The major themes of her painfully honest diary include the despair of sharing her husband with other women, her jealousy toward her rivals, and her fights with her husband. She also expressed her resentment of a society in which a woman was obliged to be dependent on her father or her husband. Because of its vivid representation of real life, the diary was influential in the work of later court ladies.

957 ▪ Birth of Akazome Emon

The Japanese court lady Akazome Emon (957–1041), one of the foremost poets of her era, was the author of at least a portion of the important historical tale *Eiga Monogatari,* the story of the powerful Fujiwara family.

c. 960 ▪ Buddhist nun Miaoshan becomes deity

The legend of Miaoshan dates from the Song dynasty (960–1279, a period of growth in Chinese literature and philosophy). Miaoshan was the earthly manifestation of the Buddhist deity Guanyin. She wanted to live a religious life, but her parents wanted her to marry. Her story had a happy ending, though: Guanyin pursued a religious vocation and converted her parents. She was one of the most important of all Chinese deities. Prayers to Guanyin on behalf of children were believed to be particularly powerful.

c. 975 ▪ Ende illustrated important manuscript

Sometime around the year 975 female painter Ende illustrated a famous copy of *The Commentary on the Apocalypse of St. John by Beatus of Liebana,* which is now located in Gerona, Spain. Her work is considered among the best in early medieval Spain. Ende apparently worked in a Spanish convent as a manuscript illuminator. She may have been a nun or a canoness (a woman who lives in a convent but is not a nun).

c. 980 ▪ Ragnilda refused marriage proposal

Around the year 980 the proud Princess Ragnilda (Rogneda), daughter of Ragvald, prince of Polatsk (a town in the area of western Russia, now in Belarus), refused to marry Prince Vladimir, who ruled the principality of Kiev (a region in western Russia, now in the Ukraine). Ragnilda scorned Vladimir because, although his father was of royal birth, his mother was a servant woman. A standard ritual in Russian marriage ceremonies required the bride to remove the boots of the groom to demonstrate his absolute dominance over her. It is said that Ragnilda did not wish to pull off the boots of a low-born man. When she refused, Vladimir took decisive action: he attacked the town of Polatsk, killed Prince Ragvald, and took Ragnilda by force.

983 ▪ Empress Adelaide helped form empire

Adelaide (Adelheid) (931–999) was the daughter of the king of Burgundy (a region in present-day France). She married King Lothar II of Italy (reigned from 946 to 950) in 947. When her husband died, she was pursued by Berengar, who wanted to claim the Italian crown. The German king Otto the Great (reigned from 936 to 973) invaded Italy to rescue Adelaide, defeated Berengar, and became king of the Lombards (members of a Germanic people who invaded a portion of Italy and established a kingdom there) and the Italians. He soon married Adelaide.

When they were crowned emperor and empress in 962 in Rome, Otto and Adelaide further united Italy and Germany in the new Roman empire. After their son Otto II (reigned from 973 to 983) died at an early age, the empire threatened to fall apart in civil war. The issue involved the rights of the young heir Otto III (reigned from 983 to 1002), Adelaide's grandson. Adelaide helped create stability by acting as coregent (substitute ruler) with her daughter-in-law, Thiophene, but Thiophene eventually forced her from power. After Thiophene's death in 991, Adelaide returned as sole regent. When Otto came of age in 996, Adelaide went into retirement.

c. 1000 ▪ "Dame Trot" wrote about childbirth

A treatise (written discussion) on childbirth and the diseases of women, written at the medical center in Salerno, Italy, sometime in the eleventh century, was widely respected throughout Europe. The treatise was signed by Trotula, whose identity is hotly debated. Some argue that Trotula was a learned female physician who taught at the center; others believe the author was actually a man. Because of the general respect given to Trotula, known popularly as "Dame Trot," other texts on obstetrics and gynecology circulated under her name until the sixteenth century.

c. 1002 ▪ Sei Shonagon composed classic book

Sei Shonagon was considered one of the most brilliant writers at a time when the literature of court ladies flourished in Japan. Her classic book *Makura no Soshi* (title means "The Pillow Book") was the first work known as *zuihitsu* ("to follow the brush"). Using a stream-of-consciousness technique (a literary method that reflects thoughts as they occur in the mind), Sei Shonagon wrote short eyewitness narratives, casual essays, impressions, lists, and imagined scenes. The title of the book came from her keeping her jottings under her pillow. *The Pillow Book* reveals the idiosyncrasies (distinct personal characteristics) of the author, giving glimpses into life at court. At one moment she is thrilled to bask in the presence of an empress whom she admires and respects; later she is ridiculing a courtier (an attendant at the royal court) whom she finds too gauche (lacking in social grace). While romantic liaisons were frequently the major topic of women's literature of this period in Japan, Sei Shonagon shows herself to be a comic artist on the subject.

c. 1008 ▪ Murasaki Shikibu wrote *Genji Monogatari*

Murasaki Shikibu, considered the greatest master of narrative prose in the history of Japanese literature, wrote *Genji Monogatari* (translated as "The Tale of Genji"). Little is known of Murasaki's life, apart from the episodes she relates in her diary, *Murasaki Shikibu nikki*. Shikibu was a lady-in-waiting to the Empress Akiko and was known at court for her writing, her knowledge of the Chinese and Japanese classics, and her proficiency with musical instru-

Middle Ages Sees a Surplus of European Women

A shortage of women seems to have existed in ancient times (beginning with earliest civilizations through the fall of the Roman empire in 476) and in the early medieval period (500–900). Women apparently began outnumbering men in Europe during the High Middle Ages (1000–1400), although this conclusion may be faulty because of a shortage of reliable data. Concerns about how unmarried women could support themselves arose during these centuries. One reason for a female surplus may have been the increasing life expectancies of women, which began to surpass those of men. They may also have benefited in general from an improved diet, which included larger quantities of iron so necessary for reproductive functions. In addition, as society became increasingly urbanized (city-centered rather than agriculturally based), women were probably less taxed by hard physical labor in fields.

The Cult of the Virgin Spans the Ages

The popularity of Mary, the mother of Jesus, among medieval Christians in Europe led to the Cult of the Virgin. Although a special position was given to Mary in the fifth century as the Mother of God, her veneration in the Roman Catholic church reached immense proportions by the twelfth century. Many cathedrals were dedicated to her, and the "Ave Maria" ("Hail Mary") came to be one of the most important prayers for Catholics. Many altar paintings also depicted her. Because the Cult of the Virgin was attacked by Protestants, it began to disappear in the sixteenth century. Nonetheless, Mary still holds an important place in the Roman Catholic and Greek Orthodox churches today.

ments. *The Tale of Genji* is a long narrative epic, featuring the romantic exploits of Prince Genji, a model of classical Japanese tastes and values. Genji is a charming, generous, and sensitive man, and it is from the depiction of his character that the book draws its strength.

1024 ▪ Gisela began influential role

Gisela (990–1043) was the daughter of the duke of Swabia (present-day West Germany) and a sister of the last king of Burgundy (an area in present-day France). Upon her father's death she inherited the duchy (a region ruled by a duke). In 1012, after her first husband, Count Bruno of Brunswick, was murdered, Gisela married her second husband, Ernst von Babenberg. Within three years Ernst died in a hunting accident, and in 1016 Gisela married Conrad, the heir to the German kingdom. This marriage was opposed by the emperor, Henry II (ruled from 1002 to 1024), as well as by church officials, who claimed the couple were too closely related to be husband and wife.

After Conrad II became the German king (reigned from 1024 to 1039), Gisela played an influential role in government. At one point she even abandoned her son from her second marriage when he rebelled against the royal government. Conrad also added Burgundy to the German empire, partly on the rights of Gisela's claims of inheritance. Gisela died four years after their son became King and Emperor Henry III (reigned from 1039 to 1056).

1035 ▪ Emma worked to gain English crown

Emma was the daughter of a Norman duke. (The Normans occupied Normandy and parts of present-day France. By

1066 they would replace the Anglo-Saxon nobility and begin a dynasty of Norman kings. The Anglo-Saxons were Germanic people who conquered England in the fifth century.) Emma married the Anglo-Saxon king Ethelred the Unready in 1002, then bore him two sons, one of whom was Edward the Confessor. A year after Ethelred's death in 1016, Emma married Canute II, the Danish king who had conquered England. With Canute she had a son named Hardecanute. Upon Canute's death in 1035, Emma worked to gain the English crown for Hardecanute and held a position of influence during his short and bloody reign (1040–1042). When Edward the Confessor became king in 1043, Emma was forced into retirement in Winchester in southern England until her death.

1040 ▪ Lady Godiva took famous nude ride

Lady Godiva (?–1080) was the wife of Leofric, Earl of Mercia, a kingdom in central England. Thirteenth-century British historian Roger of Wendover reported that in 1040 Godiva asked her husband to lower the taxes on the town of Coventry. Leofric agreed to honor her request only if she rode naked on a horse through the Conventry marketplace at midday. Godiva met his challenge, covering most of her body with her long hair. Leofric then reduced the taxes on Coventry. According to a tale that was later added to the story, Godiva asked the townspeople to stay indoors while she rode through the streets. Everyone abided by her wishes except a tailor named "Peeping Tom," who gazed upon her and was immediately struck blind. Godiva is also remembered for building and funding monasteries at Coventry and Stow.

Women Troubadours Leave Songs Behind

In southern France the twelfth century was the age of the troubadours, aristocratic poet-composers who wrote songs mainly dealing with love. As many as four hundred male troubadours are known to have existed, and historical records indicate that about twenty female troubadours ("trobairitz") have been identified. About two dozen of the women's songs survive, the last ones being composed in the early thirteenth century. Among them are four or five songs by the Countess of Dia, often called Beatrix. Although she mentions some details of her life in the vita (short biography) accompanying her songs, the information is too fragmentary to identify her positively. Through her direct and sensitive songs, Beatrix tells of her love for Count Raimbaut of Orange (whose identity is also a mystery).

1080 ▪ Birth of Matilda

Matilda (1080–1118), daughter of Malcolm III and Margaret, king and queen of the Scots, was born in 1080. She was educated in a convent under the supervision of her aunt, the abbess Cristina. In 1100 the Norman king Henry I married her to solidify his grasp of the English throne. He thought that, as a descendant of Anglo-Saxon kings, Matilda could help sway public opinion in his favor. After giving birth to a son and a daughter (the future Empress Matilda), Matilda retired from the royal court in 1103 and lived in Westminster outside London until her death in 1118. She was widely praised for her charitable works in the vicinity of London, including the founding of a leper hospital (a special hospital for people stricken with a contagious disease that deforms the body) and an Austin priory (a religious house). A learned woman, Matilda corresponded with important men of her time and patronized, or supported, writers and musicians.

1084 ▪ Poet Li Qingzhao was born

Li Qingzhao (1084–c. 1151) was a Chinese poet who excelled in a verse form called *ci*. (*Ci* are lyrical songs that are regarded in Chinese literary theory as a particularly feminine form.) Li Qingzhao was the most renowned practitioner of the *ci*. She seemed to have had a happy marriage, for many of her poems are romantic, even erotic, verses addressed to her husband.

c. 1100 ▪ Marie de France wrote feminist verse

Very little information is available about the life of Marie de France, the earliest known French woman poet. It is thought that she was born in France but lived in England, as did many French people after the Norman Conquest of 1066. (During the Norman Conquest, King Harold of England was defeated by William, duke of Normandy, who became King William I of England.) Marie may have been connected to the court of the Norman king of England, Henry II. She was famous for twelve *lais* (short narrative tales in verse) touching on all aspects of love. Marie de France has received praise from literary critics throughout the centuries for her charming style and direct expression. Modern feminist scholars are attracted to her stories because she takes the view that men and women are equal.

1118 ▪ Hélöise began love affair with Abelard

Hélöise was the niece of Fulbert, a canon (clergyman) at the cathedral in Notre Dame, France. Recognizing Hélöise's brilliance, Fulbert arranged for her to be educated at his own home by theologian and philosopher Peter (Pierre) Abelard (1079–1142). Abelard, who was in his forties at the time, was a highly regarded scholar and a popular teacher. Hélöise and Abelard fell in love and had a passionate affair. In order to conceal their relationship from Fulbert, they fled to Brittany (a region in northwestern France). After they had a son, whom they named Astralabe, they were secretly married. Soon word of the marriage reached Hélöise's family, who were angered by the news, and Hélöise took refuge in the convent at Argenteuil. Abelard did not escape their wrath, however, for he was attacked and castrated (castration is removal of the testicles) by men hired by Fulbert.

Abelard later retreated to the monastery at St. Denis, where he became a monk, and he persuaded Hélöise to become a nun at Argenteuil. He eventually gave Hélöise the Paraclete convent he had founded. Although her true devotion was to Abelard instead of God, she became the abbess (head administrator) of the convent. A record of the love affair between Hélöise and Abelard survives in their correspondence, which began when Abelard wrote *Letters to a*

The Cathar Movement Clashes With Tradition

The Cathar or Albigensian heresy (religious opinion that violated church doctrine) was popular among many Christians in the south of France, particularly women. Cathars taught that the universe is divided between good (found in spiritual things) and evil (found in material things). In order for persons to find salvation, they must lead simple and moral lives, avoiding the pleasures of the flesh as much as possible. Leadership was provided for the Cathars by the *perfecti* (the perfect ones), who practiced extreme fasting and other means of self-deprivation. At first, women could belong to the *perfecti,* although they were gradually excluded from this inner circle. Still, women were attracted to the Cathar sect because it gave them a higher status than they could hold in the Roman Catholic church. By the middle of the thirteenth century the Cathar movement was ended by a crusade mounted against them under orders of the pope (the Catholic church's head).

Eleanor of Aquitaine had five sons with Henry II, two of whom were future kings of England.

Friend. Numerous works of literature have been based on their tragic story.

c. 1119 ▪ Birth of Sun Bu-er

Chinese religious leader Sun Bu-er (1119–1183) was a matriarch (female leader) of the Quanjen school of Taoism. (Taoism is a Chinese philosophy that teaches the pursuit of harmony through appropriate action and simplicity.) Records indicate that Sun Bu-er was able to wander freely (unacceptable behavior for a woman of the upper classes of her time) by adopting the pose of a madwoman. Among her contributions to Taoism were a series of texts describing meditative practices for women. Sun Bu-er was also a skilled poet.

1137 ▪ Eleanor of Aquitaine became influential woman

Eleanor was the lively and headstrong daughter of William X, the duke of Aquitaine (an area in southwest France). In 1137 she inherited her father's vast lands, making her the most powerful woman in Europe at the time. That same year she married King Louis VII of France, and they had two daughters. After the marriage was annulled by the pope (the head of the Roman Catholic church) in 1152, Eleanor married Henry Plantagenet, duke of Normandy, who was soon to become King Henry II of England. With Henry she had three daughters and five sons, two of whom (Richard the Lion-Hearted and John) were future kings of England.

When Eleanor became estranged from Henry, she encouraged her sons to rebel against him over political matters. This action caused her to be placed under house arrest from 1174 until Henry's death in 1189. Thereafter she supported her sons, Richard I (the Lion-Hearted) and John, as kings of England. While Richard was on the Third Crusade (the Crusades were Holy Wars—military expeditions conducted by Christian powers during the eleventh, twelfth, and thirteenth centuries—

fought to defend Christianity and the church; the Third Crusade took place between 1189 and 1192), Eleanor served as regent, or substitute ruler. She managed to raise the enormous ransom demanded by the Germans for Richard's release from captivity in 1192. At the end of her long life she retired to the abbey of Fontevrault in France. Eleanor has been the subject of many books and a modern play that became the motion picture *The Lion in Winter* (1968); Katharine Hepburn won the Academy Award for best actress for her portrayal of Eleanor in the film. (*Also see entry dated c. 1170: Marie of Champagne presided at "courts of love."*)

c. 1138 ▪ Anna Comnena wrote *Alexiad*

Anna Comnena (1083–1148), the daughter of Alexius I Comnenus, emperor of the Byzantine empire, was born in Constantinople (now Istanbul, Turkey) in 1083. She was highly educated, having studied Greek, rhetoric (the art of speaking and writing effectively), philosophy, music, and science. At the age of fourteen she married Nicephorus Byrennius, a court official, with whom she had four children. After the death of Alexius in 1118, Anna's brother, John II, was to ascend the throne as their father's successor. Anna and her mother, Irene, however, led a conspiracy to prevent him from taking the crown. When their efforts failed, John retaliated by taking away their inherited property. Anna and Irene retired to a convent, where Anna devoted the remainder of her life to writing a history of the Byzantine empire. Entitled *Alexiad,* the book traces the reigns of Isaac Comnenus through Alexius (1068–1118). Many scholars consider the *Alexiad* to be superior to histories written by Latin historians. It is also regarded as one of the best histories of the First Crusade (1096–1099). (The Crusades were military expeditions conducted by Christian powers during the eleventh, twelfth, and thirteenth centuries to defend Christianity and the church.)

1141 ▪ Matilda briefly seized English throne

Matilda (1102–1167) was the daughter of King Henry I of England and his first wife, Matilda. Betrothed to the Holy Roman Emperor Henry V, she was sent to the German court at

Courtly Love Idealized Women

Courtly love idealized women in literature, if not in real life. The tradition of courtly love, a code of chivalrous behavior (acting with courtesy and honor) for medieval knights in matters of love, arose in the south of France with the troubadours (aristocratic poet-composers). The tradition moved into northern Europe largely through the influence of Eleanor of Aquitaine and Marie of Champagne. According to the rules of courtly love, a nobleman should perform great deeds to honor a noblewoman whom he loves but cannot marry. Theo-retically, he must worship his beloved from a distance, never becoming intimate with her. Although it is questionable whether the rules of courtly love were ever followed in real life, there is a vast body of medieval literature based on the courtly love ideal. In many stories, such as those about King Arthur, Queen Guinevere, and Lancelot, the lovers do commit adultery. Although women were placed on pedestals in these narratives, modern feminists question whether women were actually honored in such a way by men at that time.

the age of eight to be educated. When Matilda married Henry in 1114, she was crowned empress. After her husband's death, the English barons agreed to name Matilda the heir of Henry I as his only surviving child. In 1128 she married Geoffrey Plantagenet, soon to become count of Anjou, by whom she had three sons. When her father died in 1135, the barons reneged on, or went back on, their earlier agreement. Refusing to accept Matilda as their monarch because of her sex, they chose instead her cousin Stephen of Blois. During the civil war that followed, Empress Matilda was able to seize the throne briefly in 1141, but she was ultimately defeated. She alienated the English people with her ruthless measures to assert her power. After her eldest son became king of England as Henry II, she served as his able counselor. Matilda died in 1167. (*Also see entry dated 1080: Birth of Matilda.*)

1150 ▪ Hildegard of Bingen founded abbey

Hildegard (1098–1179) was the youngest of ten children of an aristocratic German family. At age five she had her first vision, which was perhaps connected to an illness (possibly migraines) that plagued her throughout her life. When she was eight she entered religious life by being enclosed with an anchoress (a woman who lives in seclusion for religious reasons) in a cell near the monastery of Disibodenberg. The cell eventually developed into a small convent of nuns dependent on the larger abbey. In 1136 the nuns elected Hildegard abbess (head) of the convent. When she was inspired to found a new convent in 1147, the monks of Disibodenberg resisted, fearing the loss of their own prestige (high rank; influence) and assets. Nonetheless, three years later Hildegard and about twenty nuns started a new abbey at Rupertsberg, near Bingen on the Rhine River.

At this time Hildegard also began to gain fame through her writings about her mystical visions. Her first book, *Scivias,* records prophesies and mysteries and provides instructions for the religious life. Hildegard wrote numerous other books covering such diverse subjects as theology, religious music, vices and virtues, medicines, and cures for diseases. Her wide correspondence included letters to leading figures in Europe, as well as advice for and criticisms of popes and emperors. In her lifetime she was famous throughout Christendom, even making tours in order to preach and perform exorcisms (rites performed to cast out evil spirits). She died in 1179. Although Hildegard was not officially canonized as a saint, her feast day is celebrated on September 17.

c. 1160 ▪ Herrad of Landsberg wrote *Hortus deliciarum*

Herrad of Landsberg (or Hohenburg) (1120–1195) was the abbess (head of a convent) of Hohenburg, a convent in Alsace (a former region in France). In 1160, with sixty nuns and canonesses (inhabitants of convents who do not take full religious vows) under her direction, she compiled the *Hortus deliciarum* (title means "The Garden of Delights"). The book is a richly illustrated encyclopedia covering much of the theological, historical, and scientific knowledge of Herrad's time. The oldest manuscript survives only in a modern copy; the best medieval version was destroyed during the Franco-Prussian

War, which shook the power structure in Europe from 1870 to 1871. Herrad died in 1195.

1165 ▪ Birth of Börte

Börte was the wife of Genghis Khan (1162–1227), the great Mongol (Eastern Asian) leader who ruled most of Eurasia (the name given to Europe and Asia as one continent), including northern China. She is said to have had a major influence on her husband's policy decisions. Women in Mongol society had greater authority (they could be camp, or family group, leaders) and more property rights than Chinese women.

c. 1170 ▪ Marie of Champagne presided at "courts of love"

Marie of Champagne (1145–1198) was the daughter of King Louis VII of France and Eleanor of Aquitaine. After the marriage of her parents was annulled, Marie was raised by her father. In 1164 she married Count Henry I of Champagne. Countess Marie and her mother, with whom she had maintained a close relationship, then presided over famous "courts of love" at Poitiers, France, in the 1170s. At these "courts" Marie and Eleanor conducted debates about the proper conduct of knights toward their ladies. An important literary patron, Marie of Champagne encouraged her chaplain Andreas Capellanus to write *The Art of Courtly Love*. She died in 1198. (*Also see entry dated 1137: Eleanor of Aquitaine became influential woman.*)

1180–1185 ▪ Tomoe Gozen displayed courage

Tomoe Gozen, a legendary Japanese woman warrior, is said to have displayed military skill and bravery equal to that of any man during the Taira-Minamoto War (1180–1185). According to the thirteenth-century military romance *Heike Monogatari,* Tomoe accompanied Minamoto Yoshinaka, her husband and the commander of the Minamoto forces, in battle. Yoshinaka then fled from his previous allies after they accused him of treachery and abuse of power. As one of his last surviving companions, Tomoe refused to flee for her own life until she had taken the head of an enemy warrior. It is believed that she later escaped. Her story is recounted in the play *Tomoe,* attributed to the great fourteenth-century Japanese playwright Zeami Motokiyo (c. 1363–c. 1443).

1184 ▪ Queen Tamara became sole ruler

Tamara (c. 1156–1212) was the daughter of King Giorgi III of Georgia (an Asian country on the Black Sea, south of the present-day Russian Federation). In 1178, when Tamara was nineteen, Giorgi crowned her queen and coruler. When Giorgi died in 1184 she was consecrated as the sole ruler of Georgia by the Archbishop of Kutaisi, who also proclaimed her "King of Kartli." At that time she was placed under the guardianship of her father's sister Rusundani. Three years later Tamara married George Bobolyubski, son of the Grand Prince of Kiev (a city in the Russian Ukraine), who led a life of drinking, womanizing, and waging war against the Muslims. In 1189 Bobolyubski went into exile. Tamara then married David Sosland, the prince of Ossetia (a region in Georgia). With Sosland she had a son, Giorgi, and a daughter, Rusundani.

After coming out of exile in 1191, Bobolyubski organized a group of noblemen and staged a rebellion against Tamara. After two intense battles Bobolyubski's forces were defeated, Bobolyubski was captured, and Tamara sent him to Byzantium (Turkey). He tried a second time, in 1200, to remove Tamara from the throne but was again soundly defeated. Within a few years Tamara had gained a reputation as a warrior, traveling with her troops and suffering their hardships. As they charged into battle, the men shouted, "To our king!" Tamara led daring raids into all the countries bordering Georgia—Turkey, Persia, Russia, and Armenia—killing thousands of people and bringing back even more slaves.

Medieval Midwives Gained Status

Midwifery (assistance of a woman during childbirth) was an honored profession for women in medieval times, as it was during the ancient period (beginning with earliest known civilizations through the fall of the Roman empire in 476). Typically women learned to be midwives through apprenticeships and earned handsome salaries. Midwives intervened in the birth process only when absolutely necessary, letting nature take its course. Primarily they gave psychological support to their clients. Male midwives and doctors began to replace women midwives in the seventeenth century.

1199 ▪ Hojo Masako began acquiring power

Hojo Masako (1157–1225) was the most powerful woman in medieval Japan. She was instrumental in strengthening the rule of the Kamakura Shogunate, the warrior government of medieval Japan, in which a military general (the shogun) governs on behalf of the emperor. She married Minamoto no Yoritomo in 1177, during which time Yoritomo was bringing warrior groups in Japan under his control. In 1185 he decisively defeated his enemies and became Japan's first shogun.

After Yoritomo's death in 1199, Masako took vows as a Buddhist nun, but she was nevertheless involved in the politics of choosing a successor to her husband. She served as regent (substitute ruler) first for their elder son, Yoriie, and then their younger son, Sanetomo. With the assistance of her own family, the powerful Hojo, Masako later deposed both sons for their incompetence. When her father, Emperor Tokimasa Hojo, attempted to conspire against her, she exiled him. Hojo then declared war and Masako rallied warriors to defeat his army, thus maintaining the shogunate form of military government. Known as "the nun shogun," Masako ruled the shogunate through Hojo family regents until her death in 1225.

c. 1200 ▪ Women *shirabyoshi* contributed to No drama

Performances by women *shirabyoshi* (singer-dancers) were a part of Japanese court and Buddhist temple festivities. While performing songs and dances with a strongly marked rhythm, the women were dressed in all-white male attire, wore court caps, and carried fans and swords. They were accompanied by drums and small cymbals. This form of traditional dance played an important role in the development of classical Japanese No (Noh) drama.

c. 1207 ▪ Marie d'Oignies founded Beguines

Marie d'Oignies (1176–1238) was born into a prosperous family of the Brabant, a region in the Low Countries (between present-day Netherlands and Belgium). Although she was married at the age of fourteen, she adopted a religious life in 1207

The Beguine Movement

The Beguine movement of religious life, founded by Marie d'Oignies early in the thirteenth century, began to develop in Switzerland, the Rhineland (in Germany), and the Low Countries (present-day Netherlands and Belgium). Although variations existed in their organization, all Beguines took temporary vows to live in poverty, adopt a life of chastity, and perform acts of charity in local cities. Most typically, they lived in group homes known as beguinages. The Beguines had only informal ties with the official Roman Catholic church through their confessors. Scholars suggest a major reason for development of these communities was a surplus of women during the thirteenth and fourteenth centuries. Finding it impossible to marry or enter convents without dowries (money or property), the women were attracted by the absence of a dowry requirement among the Beguines. Initially organized by well-to-do women, the sisterhood eventually included many poor women who desired shelter and economic support but lacked sincere religious motivations. As a result, the church became increasingly suspicious of the Beguines. By the fourteenth century the sisterhood was largely suppressed, although some beguinages still exist today.

with the agreement of her husband. Taking no formal vows, she gave up all her earthly possessions, became celibate (refrained from sexual relations), and engaged in charitable work among the oppressed poor. After her death in 1238 many women in northern Europe followed her example. These lay sisters of the Roman Catholic church (women who live in convents but do not take vows as nuns) came to be called Beguines. Marie d'Oignies is now known as the mother of the Beguines.

1212 ▪ Clare of Assisi cofounded "Order of Poor Clares"

Clare of Assisi (c. 1193–1235) cofounded a Franciscan convent in Assisi, Italy, with Francis of Assisi (1182–1226), founder of Franciscan monastic orders. Although Clare wanted her nuns to beg in the streets, a practice observed by Franciscan monks, the Roman Catholic church insisted that the women remain within convent walls. The "Poor Clares," as

With the help of Francis of Assisi, Saint Clare founded a Franciscan convent order called the "Poor Clares."

members of her order were known, quickly spread throughout Europe. In 1235, the year of her death, the Vatican approved Clare's rule for her order, making it the first religious rule written by a woman. Clare was named a saint in 1255.

1226 ▪ Blanche of Castile helped unify France

Blanche of Castile (1188–1252) was the daughter of the king of Castile. She married King Louis VIII of France in 1200 and bore eight living children. After her husband died Blanche served as regent (substitute ruler) for her young son Louis IX from 1226 to 1234. She ruled France again when Louis was on a crusade from 1248 to 1252, the year of her death. (The Crusades were military expeditions conducted by Christian powers during the eleventh, twelfth, and thirteenth centuries to defend Christianity and the church.) Known for her ability to manage state affairs, Blanche worked to bring stability and unity to France.

1235 ▪ Elizabeth of Hungary named saint

Elizabeth of Hungary (1207–1231) was the second daughter of King Andreas II of Hungary (reigned from 1205 to 1235). At an early age Elizabeth was betrothed to the heir of the Landgravate of Thuringia (now part of East Germany). He died before they could be married, so when she was fourteen she married his younger brother, Landgrave Ludwig IV of Thuringia (reigned from 1217 to 1227). Elizabeth lived happily with her husband and bore him three children, including a male heir. But she refused to take part in the lively court, leading a more ascetic (disciplined) and pious life and performing works of charity.

Elizabeth's path in life was influenced both by the example of Francis of Assisi (founder of the Franciscan orders, 1182–1226) and by her spiritual advisor, the papal inquisitor

Conrad of Marburg (a representative of the pope who investigated charges of heresy, religious opinions that clashed with the teachings of the church). When her husband died in Italy while preparing for a crusade (a Christian military expedition to defend Christianity and the church), her brother-in-law, Henry Raspe, seized power as regent (substitute ruler) for her son, the five-year-old heir. Eventually Elizabeth retreated to Marburg, where she became a Franciscan tertiary, a lay member of the mendicant (begging) religious order. Elizabeth dedicated the rest of her short life to fasting, prayer, and care of the sick in a hospital she founded. The church canonized her (declared her a saint) in 1235, four years after her death. Elizabeth is considered the patron saint of bakers, based on a miracle tale of her converting bread into roses.

1258 ▪ St. Mechtilde became nun

Mechtilde of Hackeborn (1241–1298) took her final vows as a nun at the age of seventeen, having entered the convent at Helfta in Saxony (a region in Germany) when she was just seven. With her beautiful singing voice, she became the convent's choir director as well as a teacher. Mechtilde was the mentor of St. Gertrude the Great and a friend of St. Mechtilde of Magdeburg. Together, they were known as the three great mystics of Helfta. In one of her revelations Mechtilde of Hackeborn is said to have heard Christ describe himself as father, mother, brother, and sister.

After Mechtilde's death in 1298, Gertrude and another nun wrote a book about Mechtilde's teaching and spiritual experiences called *The Book of Special Grace*. Her feast day is observed on November 19.

1259 ▪ Eleanor of Provence aided king

Eleanor of Provence was a daughter of the count of Provence, a powerful ruler in the south of France. She married King Henry III of England in 1236. The foreign queen was immensely unpopular because of her expensive lifestyle and her success in convincing her husband to give vast sums of money to her French relatives. Between 1259 and 1265 she secured financial aid and soldiers to help Henry subdue the English barons rebelling against his rule. After Henry's death in 1271 she continued to exert political influence by advising her eldest son, Edward I. During her final years she became a nun in the convent at Amesbury, where she died in 1291.

c. 1285 ▪ Kakusan Shido opened refuge

Kakushan Shido (1252–1306), a widow of the ruling Hojo family, established Tokeiji, a Japanese Buddhist convent. It was the best known of the *kakekomidera* (refuge temples) or *enkiridera* (divorce temples), which provided refuge for women fleeing from their husbands in the thirteenth through the nineteenth centuries. After serving in the temple for two years, a woman could be granted a divorce by the *jisha bugyo* (commissioner of shrines and temples) despite her husband's objections. The convent dealt with the women through their parents and established a special policy for processing divorces, which included obtaining a written statement of the wife's grievances; in addition, just cause (or good reason) had to be proven to finalize a divorce.

c. 1300 ▪ Novella d'Andrea lectured on law

Novella d'Andrea was born in Bologna, Italy. She was educated by her father, Giovanni d'Andrea, a professor of law at the University of Bologna. Novella frequently lectured to his classes in his absence. Because she was a female speaking at a male institution, she did not appear before her audience but was concealed behind a curtain. At that time it was feared that her beauty would distract the students.

1310 ▪ Marguerite Porète was burned at the stake

Marguerite Porète, a Beguine (a member of a lay Roman Catholic sisterhood popular in the Middle Ages) was from Hainaut, a region at the border of France and Belgium. Although little is known about her life, it is thought that between 1285 and 1295 she wrote *The Mirror of Simple Souls*. *The Mirror* describes her mystical union with God and suggests that an individual can attain salvation through faith without the assistance of priests and sacraments. In the spring of 1310 theologians at the Sorbonne in Paris condemned her writings as heretical (against the teachings of the church). Shortly thereafter, because of her beliefs, Porète was burned at the stake by the order of church authorities. Despite the church ban against it, *The Mirror* continues to be read as an anonymous work.

c. 1318 ▪ Alessandra Giliani studied blood flow

While a student at the Anatomy School in Bologna, Italy, Alessandra Giliani devised a method for studying blood flow. The technique involved injecting dye into blood vessels by drawing blood from veins and arteries and refilling them with colored liquids that later solidify. This valuable discovery enabled scientists to study the flow of blood.

c. 1322 ▪ Jacqueline Felicie accused of illegally practicing medicine

Around 1322 Jacqueline Felicie was tried and found guilty of practicing medicine without a license in Paris, France. Although there were eight witnesses testifying to the superiority of her work, the judgment went against Felicie. The Paris faculty of medicine agreed that she could not practice medicine because she had not been trained at a university. However, at that time, universities controlled the medical profession by excluding women from their campuses. Felicie was a pioneer in her profession; a woman would not become a licensed physician until the nineteenth century.

1328 ▪ Countess Loretta imprisoned archbishop

Upon the death of her husband in 1323, Countess Loretta became the regent (temporary ruler) of Sponheim, a small collection of territories on the central Moselle River in Germany. While governing until her son came of age in 1331, Loretta aggressively defended the rights of her territories against her rival, the archbishop of Trier, Baldwin von Luxemburg. In the spring of 1328 she actually captured and held the archbishop prisoner until he paid a large ransom and guaranteed her rights to properties in the area. Loretta was briefly excommunicated

Salic Law Prohibits Women from Ruling

In 1328 the French cited the Salic Law as the authority for denying the crown of France to anyone—man or woman—whose claim to the throne was traced through a woman. Passed in the early medieval period, the Salic Law prohibited women from inheriting land. The French used this means to discredit the attempt of King Edward III of England (the son of a daughter of French king Philip IV) to become their monarch when the Capetian dynasty died out with the death of Charles IV (the Fair) in 1328. Instead, Philip VI of Valois, the son of a brother of Philip IV, became the French king.

for kidnapping a cleric before being absolved by the pope at Avignon. She successfully protected her lands until her death in 1346.

c. 1330 ▪ Margaret of Tyrol married John of Innsbruck

Margaret (1318–1369) was the daughter of Henry, count of Tyrol, who was once briefly king of Bohemia (now part of present-day Czechoslovakia). When Henry sought a husband for his only legitimate child and heiress, he settled on John von Luxemburg, younger son of the reigning king of Bohemia. Twelve-year-old Margaret married the eight-year-old John of Innsbruck in 1330. When her father died five years later, Emperor Ludwig "the Bavarian" and the Austrian Habsburg family tried to seize Margaret's lands. Margaret lost Carinthia to the Habsburgs but successfully defended Tyrol. Soon, however, she tired of her husband and his relatives. In 1363 she locked John out of Castle Tyrol and told him to leave her lands forever.

Margaret then married Ludwig von Wittelsbach, the son of Emperor Ludwig of Brandenburg (now part of Poland). During their life together they experienced a series of disasters: they were excommunicated (banned from church membership) by the pope, stricken by the Black Death (bubonic plague, a bacterial epidemic disease), and attacked by the Luxemburgers. Nonetheless they managed to hold onto their lands. By 1363, however, Margaret was without an heir—both her husband and their only son had died—so she signed Tyrol over to the Austrian Habsburg dynasty.

1332 ▪ Chinese Empress Ma was born

Empress Ma (1332–1382) was the wife of Zhu Yuanzhang, the founding emperor of the Chinese Ming dynasty (or ruling family, dating from 1368 to 1644). Like her husband, she came from a poor peasant background. By the fourteenth century most elite women had bound feet (a practice that involved tightly wrapping the feet of aristocratic women to keep them very small). The empress, however, was not a member of the elite, so she had average-sized feet. This physical difference was the subject of much sensitivity. However, Ma was said to have been quite influential with her husband, exercising political power in the only way deemed appropriate for women in the late imperial period: from behind the scenes.

1346 ▪ Queen Philippa fought Scottish invaders

Philippa was the daughter of William the Good, Count of Hainaut (now part of Belgium) and Holland. At the age of 14 she married Edward III, king of England. A popular queen, Philippa was noted for her generosity toward the poor, for supporting the wool industry, and for encouraging coal mining. However, she was best known for leading English troops and defeating Scottish invaders at the Battle of Neville's Cross during her husband's absence from the continent. According to the noted historian and Philippa's friend Froissart, Philippa also joined Edward at the Siege of Calais in 1347. After the town surrendered to the English, Philippa reportedly saved the lives of six of its leading citizens by kneeling before the king and pleading on their behalf.

1346 ▪ Birgitta founded Order of St. Savior

Birgitta of Sweden was born into an aristocratic Swedish family. At the age of 14 she married the Swedish nobleman Ulf Gudmarrson. After her husband's death in 1344, she devoted herself to a life of piety and austerity (simplicity). Birgitta wrote *Revelations*, an account of her supernatural visions, which are said to have begun when she was ten years old. Because of her social position, Birgitta's advice was sought by popes, kings, and queens, who respected her mystical powers. In 1346 she founded the Roman Catholic Order of St. Savior, whose members were called Birgittines. In 1391 Birgitta was named a saint. Her daughter, St. Katarina of Sweden, was canonized (made a saint) in 1489.

c. 1377 ▪ St. Catherine helped Pope Gregory XI

Catherine of Siena (1347–1380) was born to an artisan (a craftsman) in the Italian town of Siena. At age 18 she joined the Dominican Order as a tertiary (a lay member) and dedicated herself to works of charity. Experiencing divine visions, she believed herself destined to take part in public affairs and correspond with leading men of the day. Her influence was most readily apparent by the return of Pope Gregory XI from Avignon to Rome in 1377, which restored the independence and credibility of the Roman Catholic church after 70 years. Catherine wrote a classic dialogue about her religious doctrines entitled *A Treatise on Divine Providence and 26 Prayers*. Having died in 1380, she was named a saint in 1461.

1382 ▪ Anne of Bohemia saved John Wycliffe

Anne of Bohemia (1366–1394) was the daughter of Emperor Charles IV and Empress Elizabeth of Pomerania (now part of Poland and Germany). In 1382 she married King Richard II of England. The Peasants' Revolt (a bloody rebellion in which many poor people had suffered and died) had just taken place, and Anne persuaded Richard to grant a general pardon to the participants. For this gesture she earned the love of the common people, who called her "Good Queen Anne." In 1382 she also saved the life of John Wycliffe, the English religious reformer who was condemned to death for attacking corruption in the Roman Catholic church. Anne was credited with introducing the Bohemian cap and the side saddle (a saddle for women that permits the rider to sit with both legs on one side of the horse) in England. She died in 1394 of the plague (also known as Black Death), an infectious bacterial disease that spread throughout Europe and Asia in the fourteenth century.

1384 ▪ Jadwiga began her reign at age ten

Jadwiga (1374–1399) was the daughter of Louis d'Anjou, the king of Hungary and Poland. When she was four years old she was promised in marriage to Duke William of Habsburg. Upon the death of her father in 1384 she was crowned queen of Poland. Two years later the pious (religious) young queen elected to marry Jogaila (Jagiello), the grandduke of Lithuania, as a means of converting the largely pagan Lithuanians to Christianity. The marriage established the Jagellonian dynasty, which ruled the Polish-Lithuanian union for nearly two centuries. Jadwiga reigned until she died in childbirth in 1399. Having devoted herself to helping the poor during her lifetime, she left her fortune to the revitalization of the University of Krakow.

c. 1388 ▪ Queen Margrethe became head of unified Scandinavian state

Margrethe of Denmark (1353–1412) was the daughter of the king of Denmark. In 1363 she married the king of Norway, with whom she apparently shared governing responsibilities. Upon her father's death in 1375, Margrethe ruled Denmark as regent (temporary ruler) for her young son, Olaf. Then, after her husband's death in 1380, she took over sole control of Norway in the same manner. Olaf died in 1387, and Margrethe continued her regencies in Denmark and Norway. The queen became the head of a unified Scandinavian state when the Swedes named her "Sovereign Lady and Ruler" in 1388. Noted for strengthening the royal power over the nobles, she continued in this position until her death in 1412.

c. 1390 ▪ Dorotea Bocchi taught medicine in Italy

Around 1390 Dorotea Bocchi was appointed professor of medicine at the University of Bologna, Italy. She succeeded her father in the post and remained at the university for 40 years.

c. 1393 ▪ Julian of Norwich wrote about Christ

Although details of the youth of Julian of Norwich (c. 1342–c. 1416) are scant, it is assumed she was born in Norwich, England. Some scholars believe that she lived isolated in a cell attached to St. Julian's Church wall as a recluse (one who withdraws from the world) for many years. Her wide learning, particularly in the scriptures, suggested that she had an excellent education. When she was 30, Julian experienced divine visions of Christ and the Blessed Virgin. Nearly 20 years later she wrote about them in the classic text entitled *Revelations of Divine Love.* The work attracted considerable attention because Julian wrote so profoundly on the idea of Christ as mother. Sometimes referred as an English mystic, Julian was consulted for advice throughout her lifetime because of her wisdom and divine inspirations.

c. 1399 ▪ Christine De Pisan wrote *Letters to the God of Love*

Christine De Pisan (c. 1364–c. 1431) was born in Venice, Italy. Her father was the court astrologer (one who predicts events according to the location of heavenly bodies) to King Charles V of France, where she was raised. In 1378 De Pisan married Étienne Castel, who became the king's secretary. When her husband died in 1389 she was left with three children and no income. She thus turned to writing for a living and was probably the first woman to support herself as an author.

De Pisan wrote the long poem *Letters to the God of Love,* which is viewed as the beginning of the *querelle des femmes* ("debate on women"). In *Letters,* she objects strenuously to the negative image of women in medieval literature. Christine's attack on misogyny (hatred of women) fueled the debate among literary scholars throughout Europe for centuries on the role of women. Her last poem, which she wrote at age 65, celebrated Joan of Arc's victory at Orleans, justifying her defense of women for many years. (*Also see entry dated 1429: Joan of Arc liberated Orleans, France.*)

1406 ▪ St. Colette began reforms

Colette (1381–1447) was born in Corbie, France, the daughter of a carpenter. She became a Franciscan tertiary (a person who lives in the outside world but is closely associated with a religious order) and began to live alone as a hermit at the age of twenty-one. In a vision St. Francis is said to have called her to help the Poor Clare nuns return to their original strict rule of life. Colette then spoke with the papal claimant, Peter de Luna. He was so impressed that he admitted her to the Poor Clare order and authorized her to make her reforms and to found new convents. She had no training for this work and was strongly resisted by many of the existing Poor Clare nuns. But with faith and determination, Colette persevered and over the course of 40 years founded 17 new convents and reformed several others; they are now known as the Poor Clares of the Colettine Reform and are located throughout the world. Her feast day is celebrated on March 6. (*Also see entry dated 1212: Clare of Assisi cofounded Order of Poor Clares.*)

1420 ▪ Queen Isabeau signed Treaty of Troyes

Isabeau of Bavaria (1371–1435), the daughter of the duke of Bavaria, married King Charles VI of France in 1385. The queen led a scandalous life at the dissolute (immoral) French court. Because of the king's periodic attacks of insanity, she was frequently named regent (temporary ruler). Her policies were disastrous for France, which was engaged at the time in the Hundred Years' War (1337–1453) against England. In 1420 she signed the Treaty of Troyes, by which English king Henry V was named heir of Charles VI instead of her son (later Charles VII). Charles VII's right to the throne was restored by Joan of Arc in 1429. Isabeau died in 1435 despised by both the French and English. (*Also see entry dated 1429: Joan of Arc liberated Orleans, France.*)

Joan of Arc—also called the "Maid of Orleans"— helped Charles VII in his fight for the French throne.

1429 ▪ Joan of Arc liberated Orleans, France

Joan of Arc (1412–1431) was born into a peasant family in Domrémy, France. In 1425, at the age of 13, she presented herself before Charles VII, the rightful king of France who had been denied his throne by his enemies. The English at this point were controlling most of France. Charles gave Joan permission to liberate the city of Orleans from an English siege. Wearing all-white armor, she led an advance force into Orleans, forcing the English retreat. Her military victory gave her the title of the "Maid of Orleans" and opened the way for the French to ultimately free their country from foreign domination. With a force of 12,000 troops, Joan escorted Charles through English-held territory to the cathedral at Reims for his coronation. Charles declined to support further military exploits, however, and Joan continued her military efforts independently.

In 1430 Joan was captured and sold to the British. She was then tried by an ecclesiastical court (assembly of church officials) and found guilty of a number of charges, including inappropriate physical appearance and heresy (rejection of church doctrines). Joan was burned at the stake in 1431 and canonized (declared a saint) in 1920. The story of Joan of Arc inspired a play by Maxwell Anderson, which was the basis of the film *Joan of Arc* (1948), starring Ingrid Bergman.

c. 1432 ▪ Margery Kempe dictated autobiography in English

Margery Kempe (c.1373–c.1438) was born in Lynn, England, the daughter of a well-to-do merchant. When she was 20 years old she married John Kempe, with whom she had 13 children. After the birth of her first child, Kempe suffered from acute depression but recovered when she had a direct vision of Christ. Her divine revelations, which were said to have continued until her death, usually came upon her during periods of uncontrolled weeping, often during church services. In 1413 she convinced her husband to live separately and embarked on the life of a holy woman. She went on numerous pilgrimages on the European continent. Although Kempe was illiterate, at the end of her life she dictated her autobiography, *The Book of Margery Kempe,* which has the distinction of being the first autobiography in English.

1441 ▪ Isotta Nogarola pursued sacred studies

Humanist scholar Isotta Nogarola (1418–1466) was born into a noble family of Verona, Italy. As a young woman Nogarola was trained in the new humanistic learning of the Renaissance (a revival of the arts, literature, and sciences modeled on

Greek and Roman classics), including mastery of Greek and Latin. Although some scholars praised her intellectual accomplishments, many others severely criticized her interest in secular (nonreligious) knowledge as unseemly (improper) for a woman. Therefore, when she was 23, Nogarola retreated into a "book-lined cell" in her Veronese home, where she devoted her remaining 25 years to sacred studies—more acceptable for females according to conventional wisdom of the time. She wrote many letters, orations, and treatises (written arguments that include an analysis of facts and reasoned conclusions). Nogarola's career made it clear that upper-class women of the Renaissance were encouraged to undertake humanistic studies—but not to become serious scholars.

1470 ▪ Jane Shore became mistress of Edward IV

Jane Shore (c. 1445–c. 1527) was born in London, England. At an early age she married a goldsmith, but in 1470—when she was 25—she became the mistress of King Edward IV, who was taken by her wit and beauty. Although abandoned by her husband, she was able to live in luxury with the support of the king. For 13 years, until Edward's death in 1483, Shore gained increasing political power. After the king died she was the mistress of Thomas, Lord Hasting, upon whose death she then became the mistress of the marquis of Dorset. During this time Shore continued to wield considerable influence—so much, in fact, that Edward's brother King Richard III accused her of sorcery (power gained from evil spirits). He imprisoned her in the Tower of London and later, as further punishment, forced her to become a prostitute. Toward the end of her life Shore apparently planned to marry the king's solicitor (lawyer), but the marriage did not take place and she died in poverty. *The Tragedy of Jane Shore,* a play by English poet and dramatist Nicholas Rowe, was based on Shore's life.

1479 ▪ Queen Isabella began forming united Spain

Isabella (1451–1504) was born in Castile (now part of Spain). Her father was King John II of Castile and Leon. In 1469, without the king's permission, she married Ferdinand of

Queen Isabella of Spain approved the voyage of Christopher Columbus to the New World.

Aragon (now part of Spain), with whom she had five children. In 1474 she was named queen of Castile, succeeding her brother. After her husband became king of Aragon in 1479, the couple ruled their countries together, creating a united Spain. The queen led military campaigns to end rule by the Moors (Arab conquerors of Spain) on the Iberian Peninsula (present-day Spain and Portugal), completing the task in 1492 with the conquest of Granada. That same year she approved the voyage of Christopher Columbus to the New World, which resulted in the beginning of the Spanish overseas empire. A devout Catholic, Isabella expelled both the Jews and Moors from her country to ensure that all its citizens were Christian. Her rule is best remembered for the stability it brought to Spain.

1485 ▪ Poet Veronica Gambara presided over flourishing court

Veronica Gambara (1485–1550) was born into an aristocratic Italian family. She married the count of Corregio, a tiny city-state in Italy. Widowed in 1518, the countess thereafter devoted herself to the upbringing of her two sons and the governance of Corregio. Gambara's court, over which she presided until her death in 1550, became an important center of the Italian Renaissance. (The Italian Renaissance was part of a European movement to revive the arts, literature, and sciences according to the Greek and Roman classics.) Gambara also achieved distinction as an author. Her works *The Rime* (sonnets on love and contemporary political events) and *Lettere* were published in 1759.

c. 1488 ▪ Catherine Sforza gained fame as "warrior woman"

The illegitimate daughter of the Duke of Milan, Catherine Sforza married the count of Fori-Imola, two small city-states in

Book Started Witchcraft Hysteria

In 1484 (some sources say 1485) the Roman Catholic church appointed two German priests—Henry Krämer (who took the Latin name Institoris) and Jacob Sprenger—as inquisitors (questioners) to uncover heresy (rejection of church doctrine) and disbelief among Catholics. The two pursued a special mission: finding witches. They documented their work in the book *Malleus Maleficarum* ("The Hammer of Witches"), published in 1486. This book contributed to the witch hysteria that swept over Europe and made its way to Salem, Massachusetts, in 1692.

The Hammer of Witches was an encyclopedia of contemporary knowledge about witches as well as a handbook of methods for investigating the crime of witchcraft. While acknowledging that both men and women can be tempted by the devil to use magical powers for evil, the authors maintain that women are at a greater risk of succumbing to witchcraft than men because they are more superstitious, more sexually insatiable (meaning they have greater sexual desires), more vain, and less clever than men.

According to Institoris and Sprenger, witches have the power to harm in many ways: by causing storms, slaying farm animals, killing infants in the womb, making women barren (unable to bear children), and depriving men of their "virile members" (making them impotent, or unable to engage in sexual intercourse).

northern Italy. They had six children. After her husband's assassination in 1488, Sforza governed his territory as regent (temporary ruler) for their son. Known for her vindictive (hateful or spiteful) and bloody rule, the countess led troops in battle against her enemies. For several months she bravely withstood the siege of Fori undertaken by a papal army, but capitulated to (stopped resisting) the pope's superior forces in 1500. As a result of her actions Catherine gained fame as a *virago* ("warrior woman") in fifteenth-century Italy.

1490 ▪ Beatrice d'Este presided over brilliant court

Beatrice d'Este (1475–1497) was born a member of the celebrated Este family of Ferrara, Italy. She married Lodovico "il Moro" Sforza, the duke of Milan, in 1490. For six years Beatrice ruled with her husband over Milan, which became one of the most magnificent courts of the Italian Renaissance. (The Renaissance was a European movement to revive the arts, literature, and science according to the Greek and Roman classics.)

1502 ▪ Margaret Beaufort began patronage of colleges

Margaret Beaufort (1443–1509) was the daughter of John Beaufort, England's first duke of Somerset. Marrying Edmund Tudor, Earl of Richmond, in 1455, she later gave birth to a son who would become King Henry VII in 1485. She was subsequently married to Henry Stafford in 1464 and then to Thomas Stanley, first earl of Derby in 1485. Margaret is best known as a generous patron of education. After endowing (supporting with funds) a chair in divinity at Oxford University in 1502, she established Christ College at Cambridge University (1505). In 1508 she endowed St. John's College, also at Cambridge. Oxford and Cambridge are today among the most highly regarded universities in the world. According to some accounts Margaret studied both medicine and theology and wrote books. She is also said to have lectured on writing at Cambridge.

1507 ▪ Margaret of Austria named governor of the Netherlands

Margaret of Austria (1480–1530) was born in Brussels (in present-day Belgium), the daughter of the Holy Roman Emperor Maximilian I and Mary of Burgundy. Margaret was married several times to advance Habsburg family political interests, until she became governor of the Netherlands at the age of twenty-seven. In 1483, when she was only three years old, Margaret was promised in marriage to the Dauphin of France, who soon became King Charles VIII. Charles broke the engagement, however, to make a more politically advantageous marriage with Anne of Brittany. Maximilian then promised Margaret to Prince Juan of Castile-Aragon (present-day Spain), but Juan died a few months after the wedding. Next Margaret married Duke Philibert of Savoy, with whom she enjoyed an ideal relationship until his sudden death in 1504, reportedly from a cold drink taken after an overheated hunt. Finally, Maximilian installed Margaret as governor of the Netherlands in 1507, with her own court at Mecheln. Until her death there in 1530, she was a patron of the arts and a tireless worker for peace between France and the Netherlands.

1519 ▪ Doña Marina assisted Cortés

Doña Marina (also Malinali and Malinche) came from a family in Tabasco, part of present-day Mexico on the Yucatán Peninsula. When the Spanish conquistador (conqueror) Hernán Cortés and his army invaded Tabasco in 1519, she served as a Tabascoan slave named Malinali. She spoke not only Mayan (the language of the Tabascoans) but also Nahuatl, the language of the Aztecs (the ruling dynasty). Because of Malinali's linguistic abilities the Spaniards chose her as a translator. Baptized and named Doña Marina by the Spaniards, she became Cortés's "voice" with the native people, who called them both "Malinche."

Fifteen-year-old Marina was also Cortés's mistress, traveling with him and serving as his advisor and even his spy. For instance, she informed Cortés of a plot to annihilate the Spanish army at Cholula (an Aztec town in southeast Mexico). Cortés then gathered 6,000 Cholulan warriors in the town square and mowed them down with gunfire. In addition, Marina was the translator at a 1519 meeting between Cortés and Aztec king Montezuma II at the Aztec capital, Tenochtitlán (present-day Mexico City).

By 1521 Cortés had conquered the Aztec empire and founded New Spain. The next year Marina gave birth to Cortés's son, whereupon Cortés gave her land, gold, and servants (although he sent for his wife to join him in New Spain).

1519 ▪ Isabella d'Este supported Italian Renaissance

Isabella d'Este (1474–1539) was a member of the celebrated Este family of Ferrara, Italy. In 1490 she married Francesco Gonzaga, the marquis of Mantua, by whom she had six children. Possessing great diplomatic skill, the marchioness (wife of a marquis) took an active role in Mantua's government. When her husband died in 1519, she became a trusted advisor to her eldest son, who took over control of the city-state. Isabella is chiefly remembered for her role in supporting the Italian Renaissance (a revival of art, literature, and science modeled on the Greek and Roman classics) by being the patron of artists and intellectuals in Mantua.

1525 ▪ Catherine von Bora married Martin Luther

Catherine (Katherine) von Bora (1499–1552) took vows as a nun when she was 16 years old. In 1523 the church reform ideas of the German monk Martin Luther reached her convent. (Luther attacked corruption in the Roman Catholic church, ultimately bringing about the Protestant Reformation and the founding of Lutheranism, the first Protestant denomination, or group of religious congregations.) Von Bora and eight other nuns eventually ran away from the convent. Uncertain how to live on her own, von Bora offered to marry Luther himself, who was 16 years older than she. At first surprised, the great reformer accepted her proposal and they were married four weeks later.

Catherine von Bora became a model wife and mother and a capable manager. She took over Luther's busy household in his former monastery, raised several of his nephews, and bore three sons and three daughters. Widowed in 1546, Catherine died six years later while fleeing religious persecutors.

c. 1525 ▪ Argula von Grumbach supported Lutheranism

Argula von Stauffer Grumbach (1492–1563) was born into a noble family in Bavaria (a German state). When she was ten years old her parents died, and she was taken to the court of Duke William of Bavaria, who became her protector. In 1516 she married Frederick von Grumbach, with whom she had four children. Her public support of the cause of Protestantism (a movement for reform of the Roman Catholic church initiated by Martin Luther) brought condemnation from Catholics and opposition from her family. Yet Grumbach also gained considerable support from Protestants and met with Martin Luther in 1530. After her husband's death that same year, she was briefly married, then widowed a second time. Grumbach spent the rest of her life on her estates. The duke of Bavaria imprisoned her for a short time in 1563 because she persisted in circulating books and ideas contrary to the Catholic religion.

1527 ▪ Marguerite of Navarre encouraged Renaissance culture

Marguerite of Navarre (1492–1547) was born into the French royal family. Her close relationship with her brother, King Francis I, made her one of the most influential women in France during the sixteenth century. In 1527 she married Henry II, king of Navarre (a region in southwest France). At her court Marguerite encouraged Renaissance culture (a revival of art, literature, and science modeled on Greek and Roman classics). She was not only a literary patron but also an author herself, writing plays, poems, stories, and spiritual meditations. Marguerite's most famous work is the *Heptaméron*, a collection of 72 short stories.

1533 ▪ Catherine of Aragon won admiration

Catherine of Aragon (1485–1536) was the daughter of Ferdinand of Aragon and Isabella of Castile. In 1501 Catherine married Arthur, Prince of Wales, heir to the British throne. He died six months later, and she was soon betrothed to Arthur's brother, 11-year-old Henry. Catherine and Henry were married in 1509, when he became Henry VIII, king of England. The couple had four children, of whom only a daughter, Mary I, survived infancy. In 1527 Henry requested an annulment of their marriage because he wanted a male heir to the throne and Catherine was then past childbearing age. He had also decided to marry Anne Boleyn, a beautiful young court attendant. The pope, as head of the Roman Catholic church, denied Henry's request, which violated the doctrine against divorce or dissolution of a church-sanctified (blessed) marriage. Catherine herself did not want an annulment (a pronouncement that a marriage is invalid, or never really took place in the eyes of the church), and she resisted in a dignified manner that gained her the love of the English people.

In 1533, after Henry secretly married Anne, the archbishop (the pope's representative) approved the annulment. The following year, however, the pope decided Catherine's marriage to Henry was indeed valid; as a result Henry made his famous break with the Catholic church to establish the Church of England. During this time Catherine had gone into retirement at a palace in Bedfordshire. She refused to accept the title of princess dowager (dowager is a term used for an elderly woman), nor would she acknowledge the Act of Succession (1534), which declared her daughter Mary illegitimate. The story of Henry VIII and Anne Boleyn is retold in the film *Anne of the Thousand Days* (1969). (*Also see entry dated 1479: Queen Isabella began forming a united Spain; 1536: Anne Boleyn was beheaded; and 1553: "Bloody Mary" tried to reestablish Roman Catholicism.*)

c. 1535 ▪ Angela Merici founded Company of St. Ursula

Angela Merici (1474–1540) founded the Company of St. Ursula in Brescia, Italy. It was a religious congregation of non-cloistered women (they did not take vows as nuns) dedicated to teaching girls. At first the Ursulines lived in their homes and engaged in prayer and charitable activities. In 1626, however, they were forced by the Roman Catholic church to become nuns and live in cloisters (an area in a convent secluded from the outside world). Eventually they achieved wide recognition for their superior methods of educating girls. Angela Merici was named a saint in 1807. Ursuline schools for girls still exist throughout the world.

1536 ▪ Anne Boleyn was beheaded

Anne Boleyn (1504–1536) was born in England, the daughter of Sir Thomas Boleyn and Elizabeth Howard. After being educated for several years at the French court, she returned to England. When she attended the court of the king, Henry VIII, she caught his eye. In 1533 Henry succeeded in convincing the Roman Catholic church to annul his marriage to his first wife, Catherine of Aragon. He then married Boleyn, hoping she could produce a male heir to the throne. Later that year Boleyn gave birth to a daughter, the future Elizabeth I. When she had a stillborn son in January 1536, Henry turned against her and charged her with infidelity and treason. Imprisoned in the Tower of London, Boleyn was convicted by a prejudiced court and beheaded the following May. Within 11 days Henry married his third wife, Jane Seymour. The story of Henry VIII and Anne Boleyn was retold in the film *Anne of the Thousand Days* (1969). (*Also see entry dated 1533: Catherine of Aragon won admiration; 1537: Jane Seymour gave Henry VIII male heir; and 1558: Queen Elizabeth I began her reign.*)

Anne Boleyn, the second wife of England's King Henry VIII, was the mother of Elizabeth I.

1537 ▪ Jane Seymour gave Henry VIII male heir

Jane Seymour (1509–1537) was born in England, the daughter of John Seymour, a soldier. She served as a lady-in-waiting (someone who waits on the queen) to Catherine of Aragon, the first wife of Henry VIII. She was also a lady-in-waiting to Henry's second wife, Anne Boleyn, when Henry had Boleyn beheaded in 1536. Eleven days after the execution Seymour became the king's third wife. In 1537 she gave birth to a son, Edward, Henry's long-awaited male heir. Seymour died 12 days later. Upon the death of Henry VIII in 1547, their son became King Edward VI, but he did not live beyond his sixteenth year. (*Also see entry dated 1533: Catherine of Aragon won admiration; and 1536: Anne Boleyn was beheaded.*)

1538 ▪ Vittoria Colonna published her first collection

Vittoria Colonna (1492–1547) was born in Marino, Italy, into a noble family. In 1509 she married the marquis of Pescara, thus becoming a marchesa and moving to Naples. She

English queen Jane Grey held the royal title for only nine days before Mary Tudor, a Catholic, took the throne.

rarely spent time with her husband, who was in the military. After he died in 1525, Colonna lived in various convents, but she never became a nun. She had many influential acquaintances, including high officials in the Roman Catholic church. Her most celebrated friend was the Italian artist Michelangelo, with whom she exchanged letters and poems. Colonna pressed vigorously for reform in the Catholic church, although she never accepted Protestantism (a Christian sect that broke away from Catholicism). A collection of her poetry, published in 1982, includes 390 pieces. They reveal Colonna's deep spirituality and considerable learning.

1542 ▪ Mary crowned Queen of Scots

Mary (1542–1587) was born in Lilithgow, Scotland, the daughter of James V of Scotland and Mary of Guise. Her two older brothers both died in infancy. Mary's father died when she was a few days old, making her the sole heir to the crown of Scotland. She was crowned queen while still an infant and held the title from 1542 until 1567.

Mary of Guise (Mary's mother) served as regent (temporary ruler) for her daughter, who was sent at the age of five to France to be raised at the court of Henry II. Mary married Francis, the heir to the French throne, in 1558 and served as queen consort (coruler) of France briefly before her husband's death in 1560. She returned to Scotland the next year. (*Also see entry dated 1587: Mary Stuart was executed.*)

1546 ▪ Artist Lavina Teerlic enjoyed successful career

Lavina Teerlic (1520–1576) was born in Flanders (now part of Belgium and France). A painter of miniatures (small portraits and pictures), she was appointed the court miniaturist for King Henry VIII of England. By 1546 Teerlic's yearly income was higher than that of Hans Holbein, a famous German painter.

1553 ▪ Lady Jane Grey ruled England for nine days

Jane Grey (1537–1554) was born in Bradgate, Leicestershire, England. She was the daughter of Henry Grey, the marquess of Dorset, and Frances Brandon and the great-granddaughter of King Henry VIII. Jane was raised a Protestant and educated by the bishop of London (head of the Anglican church—established by King Henry VIII—in the city). When 16-year-old King Edward VI (the son of Henry VIII and Jane Seymour) lay dying, Jane was married against her will to Lord Guildford Dudley. Guildford's father, the earl of Warwick, had arranged the marriage to ensure that a Protestant took the throne after the death of Edward, who was also a Protestant. After Edward died in 1553 Jane was named queen of England, but she held the title for only nine days before Mary Tudor, a Catholic, took the throne as Mary I. In 1554 Jane and her husband were executed for high treason at the order of the queen. The story of Jane Grey was adapted as a 1985 British film titled *Lady Jane,* starring Helena Bonham Carter. (*Also see entry dated 1553: "Bloody Mary" tried to reestablish Roman Catholicism.*)

Mary Tudor persecuted Protestants in an ill-fated attempt to destroy the Anglican church.

1553 ▪ "Bloody Mary" tried to reestablish Roman Catholicism

Mary Tudor (1516–1558) was the daughter of King Henry VIII of England and his first wife, Catherine of Aragon. When Henry arranged the annulment of his marriage to Catherine and established the Anglican church (Church of England) in 1533, Mary remained loyal to her Catholic mother. Henry then forced her to sign a declaration that her mother's marriage had been unlawful.

After Mary's half-brother, King Edward VI (the son of Henry VIII and his third wife, Jane Seymour), died in 1553,

Mary was entitled to the crown. The Duke of Northumberland, however, wanted to prevent Mary from taking the throne because she was a Catholic. Before Edward's death, Northumberland persuaded Edward to set Henry's will aside and make Lady Jane Grey next in line for the throne. Grey was a Protestant, and with her as queen the Anglican church (Church of England) would be assured of remaining in power. Grey reigned briefly—nine days—before Mary, who had gained popular support, arrived in London to claim the crown.

Mary had Northumberland and two of his associates executed, for the moment sparing the lives of Grey and her husband, Lord Guildford Dudley. (Mary, however, did have them put to death the following year.) Mary then gained the throne, becoming Mary I of England. During her five-year reign, she persecuted Protestants in a futile attempt to destroy the Anglican church and reestablish Roman Catholicism in England. Because nearly 300 Protestants were killed during this time, she became known as "Bloody Mary." In 1554 she married Philip II, king of Spain. Mary died childless four years later. (*Also see entry dated 1533: Catherine of Aragon won admiration; and 1553: Lady Jane Grey ruled England for nine days.*)

1554 ▪ Gaspara Stampa left important poems

Gaspara Stampa (1524–1554) was born in Padua, Italy, into a middle-class family. She spent most of her short life in Venice, where she was a courtesan (a prostitute and intellectual companion for wealthy men). After Stampa died in 1554 her lyric love poems were published by her sister. Stampa had written sonnets (14-line poems) in the style of the great Italian poet Petrarch. (Known as the Petrarchan or Italian sonnet, the first eight lines have a fixed rhyme scheme, while the remaining six lines have a variable rhyming pattern.) Telling the story of Stampa's betrayal by a lover in Venice, the passionate poems indirectly mock men and challenge the ideas of the time. Stampa's poetry gained new appreciation during the nineteenth century, when she was compared to the Greek female poet Sappho (*Also see entry dated c. 610 B.C.: Sappho wrote poetry.*)

c. 1555 ▪ Louise Labé wrote notable love sonnets

Louise Labé (1525–1565) was born in Parcieux, France, the daughter of a wealthy ropemaker. Labé was well educated. She studied Latin and music and became a skilled horseback rider. According to some accounts, she disguised herself as a knight and fought in a battle at Perpignan, France. In 1550 she married Ennemond Perrin, who was a ropemaker (like her father) in Lyons. Labé was then known as "la Belle Cordière" (the lovely ropemaker). She formed a literary circle in her home, which became a center for French Renaissance poets. (The French Renaissance was a revival of art, literature, and science modeled on the Greek and Roman classics.) Five years later Labé published *Oeuvres* ("Works"), a collection of elegies (poems expressing sorrow or lamenting the death of a beloved person) and Petrarchan sonnets (a 14-line poem originated by the Italian poet Petrarch, with the first eight lines having a fixed rhyme scheme and the last six lines having a variable rhyming pattern). In 1555 Labé completed another famous work, *Débat de folie et d'amour* ("Debate between Folly and Love"). She was also known as a strong advocate of higher quality education for women.

c. 1557 ▪ Religious teacher Tanyangzi was born

Tanyangzi (c.1557–1580) was born into an elite family in Suzhou, China. She became a religious educator, combining elements of Daoism, Buddhism, and Confucianism in her teachings. (Taoism is a Chinese mystical philosophy that advocates a life of harmony. Buddhism, which was founded by the Indian philosopher Siddhãrta Gautama—known as the Buddha—stresses liberation from suffering through mental and moral self-purification. Confucianism is a social philosophy founded by the Chinese philosopher K'ung Fu-tse—Confucius—that promotes peace through moral social structures.) Tanyangzi's method was typical of the syncretic (harmonizing) thought of her time. She is said to have ascended heavenward and attained immortality in broad daylight. Tanyangzi attracted as her disciples a number of men from prominent families, who wrote numerous volumes about her.

Elizabeth I of England is credited with turning England into a major European power.

1558 ▪ Queen Elizabeth I began her reign

Elizabeth Tudor (1533–1603) was the daughter of King Henry VIII of England and his second wife, Anne Boleyn. She was well educated and brought up in the Protestant faith. In 1537 Henry's third wife, Jane Seymour, gave birth to Edward (later King Edward VI), the male heir to the throne. Elizabeth and her half-sister, Mary Tudor (the Roman Catholic daughter of King Henry VIII and his first wife, Catherine of Aragon), were then declared illegitimate by an act of Parliament.

When Edward VI died in 1553, Elizabeth defended Mary's claim to the throne against those who supported the Protestant Lady Jane Grey as queen. After Mary became queen, though, she became mistrustful of Elizabeth's Protestantism, so she had Elizabeth imprisoned in the Tower of London. Upon Mary's death in 1558, Elizabeth became queen of England. Her long period of reign, which continued until her own death in 1603, has often been called the "Elizabethan Age."

Known as the "Virgin Queen," Elizabeth once explained in a speech to Parliament her decision to remain unmarried: "I have long since made choice of a husband, the kingdom of England . . . ." She supported the Protestants by restoring the Anglican church, thereby reversing the Roman Catholic policies of Mary I. In 1587 Elizabeth learned of several Catholic plots to remove her from the throne and replace her with Mary Stuart, queen of Scots, who was a Catholic. Elizabeth then approved the execution of Mary on charges of treason later in 1587.

During this time Spain (a Catholic country) had become involved in undermining Elizabeth's rule. In 1588, however, Elizabeth's position was secured when the English defeated the Spanish Armada (a vast fleet of powerful warships), which was sent to invade England. Under Elizabeth's guidance England emerged as a major European power. (*Also see entry dated 1536: Anne Boleyn was beheaded; 1537: Jane Seymour gave Henry VIII male heir; 1542: Mary crowned Queen of Scots; 1553: "Bloody Mary" tried to reestablish Roman Catholicism; 1553: Lady Jane Grey ruled England for nine days; and 1587: Mary, Queen of Scots, was executed.*)

1559 ▪ Sofonisba Anguissola appointed Spanish court painter

Sofonisba Anguissola (c. 1535–1625) was born in Cremona, Italy. Her father decided to educate his six daughters on the same level as his only son. This decision contrasted sharply with the view of the day—that women ought to be prepared only for domestic duties. Consequently, Anguissola was able to develop her considerable talent for painting under capable instructors, such as the Italian master Michelangelo, who encouraged her artistic career. Establishing a reputation as a fine portraitist, Anguissola went to Spain in 1559 at the invitation of King Philip II to serve as painter for the Spanish court. She remained in Spain until 1580, when she married and moved to Sicily. After her husband's death, she married again and lived to be ninety. At least 50 of her works, most of them portraits, still exist.

1559 ▪ Duchess of Parma named governor of Netherlands

Margaret von Habsburg (1522–1586) was the illegitimate daughter of Holy Roman Emperor Charles V and a mistress, Jean van den Gheynst. Margaret's father first married her off to Alexander de Medici in 1536. When de Medici was murdered a year later she briefly took over the government in Florence, Italy. In 1538 Margaret married Ottavio Farnese, who became duke of Parma. Farnese quarreled with Charles, however, and became an ally (partner or supporter) of the king of France.

The successor of Charles V, Margaret's half-brother King Philip II of Spain, named her governor of the Netherlands in 1559. Margaret was soon caught between quarreling groups of nobles and bureaucrats (government officials, especially ones who follow a narrow and rigid set of rules) and had to deal with the ongoing religious clash between Catholics and Protestants, but still she managed to assert her authority. A staunch Catholic, she suppressed a revolt by Calvinists (a Protestant sect). She resigned in 1567 when the duke of Alba and his army, sent by Philip, brought brutal oppression to the Netherlands. Philip reinstated Margaret as governor in 1580, although she had to share power as governor with her son, Alexander Farnese. Again dissatisfied with the limits on her authority, Margaret withdrew from the government three years later.

1562 ▪ Teresa of Ávila founded Discalced Carmelites

Teresa (1515–1582) was born into an aristocratic family in Ávila, Old Castile (Spain). When she was 21 she entered the Carmelite (an order of Roman Catholic nuns) convent in her home town. During middle age she underwent a religious awakening and began having mystical visions. Teresa decided to lead a reform of the Carmelites, eventually establishing 16 convents of the Discalced, or Barefoot, Carmelites, who live under a rule of extreme austerity (self-discipline). She wrote a number of works about her experiences, the most notable being her autobiography, *Las moradas* (1577; "The Interior Castle"), which describes the soul as a castle with many rooms. Her last book, *Libro de las fundaciones* (1610; "The Book of Foundations"), provides a detailed account of life in the late sixteenth and early seventeenth centuries.

1564 ▪ Maharanee Durgawati died at Battle of Narhi

Maharanee Durgawati became ruler of Gondwana (a region in India) when her husband died in 1548. She was a compassionate leader, renowned for her great beauty and even greater military skill. The role of elite women in India was in transition during the sixteenth century, and females began exerting more and more independence in the spheres of politics and warfare. Like her male predecessors, Durgawati enlarged her territory through military conquest.

In 1562 Akbar the Great ascended to the throne of the Mogul (Mughal) empire. (The Mughals were a Muslim dynasty, or ruling family, in India. The Muslims are believers in

Islam, a religion founded by the Prophet Muhammad in Asia in the eighth century.) Two years later a Mogul army invaded Gondwana, and the opposing forces engaged in a destructive cycle of heated pursuit, near capture, and escape. As Durgawati's forces marched to the mountain village of Narhi, Mogul troops seized the mountain passes. Leading a counterattack, Durgawati drove out the enemy. She then planned a nighttime surprise attack, but the majority of her chiefs rejected the tactic. As a result, the next day the Moguls easily recaptured the cliffs. Leading her outnumbered army into battle, Durgawati successfully opposed three Mogul attacks. On the second day of battle, however, her army was overwhelmed. Wounded and fearing capture, she took her own life. After the defeat Gondwana was absorbed into the Mogul empire.

1572 ▪ Catherine de Médicis took part in massacre

Catherine de Médicis (1519–1589) was born in Florence, Italy, the daughter of the duke of Urbino. In 1533, when she was 14, she married Henry, Duke of Orleans, with whom she had four sons and five daughters. Henry became king of France in 1547 (and was known thereafter as Henry II). Although Catherine was the queen, Henry neglected her in favor of his mistress, Diane de Potriers, from whom he sought affection as well as advice on ruling his kingdom.

When Henry died in 1559, Catherine served as regent (temporary ruler) for her young sons Francis II (the first husband of Mary, Queen of Scots) and Charles IX until 1574. While Charles was on the throne, a power struggle erupted between the dominant Catholics and the Protestant Huguenots (1562–1569) in France. (The Huguenots followed the teachings of religious reformer John Calvin.) At first Catherine tried to maintain peace by balancing support of the opposing groups.

Catherine de Médicis approved the infamous massacre of Protestants on St. Bartholomew's Day in 1562.

Finally, however, she approved the infamous massacre of Protestants on St. Bartholomew's Day in 1562. Despite this bloody move, she is credited with holding France together during a period of intense internal conflict. Catherine's influence decreased during the reign of her son, Henry III (1574–1589).

1573 ▪ Sophia Brahe calculated eclipse

Sophia Brahe (1556–1643) was a Danish student of astronomy (the study of matter found outside Earth's atmosphere). In 1573 she assisted her brother, the famous astronomer Tycho Brahe (1546–1601), in observations leading to their calculation of the lunar eclipse. (During the lunar eclipse, the moon is darkened by Earth's shadow.) Sophia continued to help her brother frequently in his astronomy research, and she also became an excellent horticulturist (one who studies the growing of plants).

1583 ▪ Tarquinia Molza joined musicians' group

Tarquinia Molza (1542–1617) was a popular singer in Italy during the Renaissance, a period lasting from the fourteenth to the seventeenth century during which art and literature flourished. In addition to singing, she composed musical pieces for voice, lute, viol, and harp. From 1583 to 1589 Molza was a member of a group of four "lady singers" organized by the Duke of Ferrara at his court. She was eventually dismissed from this celebrated group—one of the first professional groups for female musicians—because of her scandalous lifestyle.

1586 ▪ Mary Sidney published poems

Mary Sidney (c. 1561–1621) was born into an aristocratic family in England. At age 16 she married Henry Herbert, the earl of Pembroke. Throughout her life she was always close to her brother, noted English poet Sir Philip Sidney, and she developed a deep interest in literature. As the countess of Pembroke, Mary Sidney became a great patron of learning. After her brother's death in 1586, she edited and published his poems. Her most notable accomplishment was the completion of his translation of the Psalms (sacred poems) into English.

1587 ▪ Yodogimi became concubine

Yodogimi (c. 1567–1615) was the daughter of Odani no Kata, who was herself a victim of marriage politics. At the age of 20, Yodogimi became the "bedtime attendant," or concubine, of 51-year-old Toyotomi Hideyoshi. Hideyoshi was a military leader who wanted to unify Japan under his authority. While Hideyoshi is said to have treated Yodogimi well, he was nevertheless responsible for the deaths of her mother, stepfather, and brothers. Around 1590 Yodogimi gained power over Hideyoshi as the mother of his only child, a male heir. The child died at the age of two, but Yodogimi later gave birth to another son, Hideyori. Hideyoshi died in 1598, when the boy was still young. Yodogimi then successfully rallied (joined together supporters of a common cause) allies of the Toyotomi family to back the rise of her son, Hideyori, to power. In 1615, however, enemy forces besieged their castle, and Yodogimi and Hideyori committed suicide.

Mary, Queen of Scots, was kept under house arrest for 18 years by Queen Elizabeth I of England.

1587 ▪ Mary, Queen of Scots, was executed

Mary Stuart (1542–1587), known as Mary, Queen of Scots, was kept under house arrest for 18 years by Queen Elizabeth I of England. A first cousin to Mary, who was a Roman Catholic, Elizabeth became aware of Catholic plots to give the English crown to the Queen of Scots. Elizabeth had supported Protestantism in England throughout her reign. In 1587 she approved the beheading of Mary Stuart in order to protect her own position. In 1603 James I—the son of Mary, Queen of Scots—succeeded Elizabeth I to the English throne. The story of Mary Stuart was dramatized in a play by Maxwell Anderson, which served as the basis for the 1936 film *Mary of Scotland,* starring Katharine Hepburn. (*Also see entry dated 1558: Queen Elizabeth I began reign.*)

Salon Society Offered Educational Opportunities

Salon society, in which hostesses held receptions in their salons (drawing rooms) for the purpose of intellectual conversation, was originated by Madame de Rambouillet in Paris, France, early in the seventeenth century. Spreading from France throughout Europe, salon society flourished during the seventeenth and eighteenth centuries. Both men and women of aristocratic and bourgeois (middle-class) backgrounds participated in the salon experience. Salon society offered women opportunities for extending their education through intellectual exchange. The *saloniéres* (women of the salons) were often ridiculed for aspiring to rise above their traditional place in the domestic sphere. In England women who pursued intellectual interests were called "bluestockings," a term that carried negative connotations.

c. 1588 ▪ Madame de Rambouillet was born

Catherine de Vivonne (c. 1588–1665) was born into the French nobility. At the age of 12 she married Charles d'Angennes, who became Marquis de Rambouillet. Disgusted with the crude and unrefined state of the French court in the early seventeenth century, Madame de Rambouillet established a salon, or meeting place, in her Parisian townhouse to help restore elegance, style, and intellectualism to high society. She was hostess to members of the aristocracy—both male and female—as well as men of learning, who met to engage in serious conversation, particularly on literary matters. Madame de Rambouillet had a great influence on the development of French literature. After her death in 1665, salon society flourished in France and other European countries.

1590 ▪ Novelist Maria de Zayas was born

Maria de Zayas (1590–1661) was born into a noble family in Madrid, Spain. Little is known of her life, although it is thought that she lived in Zaragoza because her novels were published there. de Zayas is considered the most important of the minor Spanish novelists of the seventeenth century. In her works—which were widely read in her time—de Zayas criticized the subjugation (being under the control of another; in this case, women being subjected to the authority of men) of women in Spanish society.

c. 1591 ▪ Veronica Franco opened women's shelter

Veronica Franco (1546–1591) was an Italian Renaissance poet. (The Italian Renaissance was part of an artistic revival throughout Europe following the end of the medieval period and continuing until modern times.) Franco opened a refuge, or shelter, for women of the streets in Venice, Italy. Her poetry was neglected for centuries, but she is now known as an able writer who was profoundly concerned with women's social issues.

c. 1599 ▪ Beatrice Cenci beheaded

Beatrice Cenci (1577–1599) was the daughter of Francesco Cenci, a Roman nobleman who was known for his cruelty. In 1595, when Beatrice was 18 years old, her father imprisoned her in a castle with her stepmother, Lucrezia. Seeking revenge, Beatrice, Lucrezia, and Beatrice's brothers arranged the murder of Francesco. The conspirators were all arrested and found guilty in a famous trial in 1599. They were beheaded by order of Pope Clement VIII. The tragic story of beautiful Beatrice and her family inspired English poet Percy Bysshe Shelley to write the dramatic play *Cenci* (1819).

1600 ▪ Hon-Cho-Lo, the "Terror of the Yangtze"

Hon-Cho-Lo was born in China. She gained notoriety for her pirating activities in the early seventeenth century after the death of her husband, who was also a pirate. Taking command of his ship, Hon-Cho-Lo became known as the "Terror of the Yangtze" as she preyed upon vessels sailing on the 3,434-mile river that crosses the entire width of China.

c. 1603 ▪ Izumo no Okuni started *kabuki* theater

Izumo no Okuni (1572–?) was an attendant at Izumo Shrine, a major Shinto center. (Shinto was the official religion of Japan.) She later achieved acclaim as the leader of a success-

Geisha and Prostitutes Licensed

In order to maintain standards of public morality, the Japanese government set aside parts of the cities of Kyoto (Shimabara) and Edo (Yoshiwara), where *geisha* (artists and entertainers) and prostitutes congregated in walled areas. The women were licensed to entertain men in restaurants and tea houses. *Geisha* were trained in traditional dance and music, and they were skilled in the arts of charm and conversation. *Yujo* ("women of pleasure"), on the other hand, were more clearly prostitutes. While the licensing of pleasure quarters ended with the fall of the government in 1868, the practices continued into modern times. Feminists successfully worked to make prostitution legal in Japan in 1957.

Witch Hunts Spread

During the sixteenth and seventeenth centuries, the witch hunts that began in Europe in the fifteenth century gained momentum, eventually reaching the New England colonies in America. The last recorded witchcraft trial in Western Europe took place in Glaris, Switzerland, in the eighteenth century, when Ann Goeldi was hanged for allegedly casting spells on a doctor's son. Throughout the more than 300 years of the witchcraft hysteria, hundreds of people were executed, most of them women. Sometimes entire families were killed.

ful women's theater troupe. Performing in Kyoto in 1603, her troupe combined current songs and dances with popular fashion and dramas in which the women impersonated men. Known as *Okuni kabuki,* the performers were soon imitated by other groups of itinerant (traveling) female entertainers. The Japanese government suppressed the performances, however, and eventually prohibited women from appearing on stage because they were thought to offend public morality.

1603 ▪ Lavinia Fontana became court painter

Lavinia Fontana (c. 1552–1614), who excelled in painting portraits and religious scenes, was born in Bologna, Italy. Her father, a painter named Prospero Fontana, taught her his craft. Lavinia married Gian Paolo Zappi, a fellow student in her father's studio. Zappi eventually gave up his own career to care for the couple's numerous children and allow Lavinia time for painting. She gained prominence throughout Italy for her portraits and religious scenes and in 1603 moved with her family to Rome to become one of the official painters of the papal (relating to the pope or the Roman Catholic church in general) court. There are 135 known works by Lavinia Fontana.

1606 ▪ St. Rose of Lima dedicated life to religion

Isabel de Flores y del Oliva (1586–1617), also known as Rosa, was born to poor Spanish parents in Lima, Peru. She worked hard to help support her family by growing and selling flowers and doing needlework. Rosa refused to marry, and at age 20 she became a Dominican tertiary (a person who lives in the regular, lay world but is closely associated with an order of monks). Living in a summerhouse in her parents' garden, she spent long hours praying and inflicting severe penances on herself. Rosa also devoted her energy to caring for the sick and poor as well as Indians and slaves. Named St. Rose of Lima by the Catholic church in 1671, she is considered the founder of social service in Peru. She is also the patron saint of all South America.

c. 1607 ▪ Francesca Caccini was court musician

Francesca Caccini (1587–1640) came from an Italian family of distinguished musicians. Although she was born and lived in Florence, Italy, she made her first singing appearance at court in Tuscany (a region in France) in 1600. Caccini enjoyed a long professional career as a singer and composer, serving the Tuscan court as a highly paid musician from 1607 to 1627. In addition to singing, she played the lute, guitar, and harpsichord. Caccini also composed music, her most famous work being the opera *La liberazione di Ruggiero*. After her first husband died in 1626, she may have married again.

1607 ▪ Novelist Madelaine de Scudéry was born

Madelaine de Scudéry (1607–1701) moved to Paris, France, at a young age to join her brother, successful dramatist Georges de Scudéry, who was living there. She held a literary salon in her home, establishing herself as a successful hostess and gaining fame as a writer. Madame de Scudéry's lengthy novels about Paris society were extremely popular because the characters were based on important figures who were easily recognized by her readers. Treasuring her own independence by remaining single, she advocated the education of women— and voiced this opinion frequently in her novels. Although her works are no longer widely read, Madame de Scudéry had an impact on the development of the novel, particularly because of her masterful character analysis.

1607 ▪ Pocahontas saved John Smith

Pocahontas (c. 1595–1617) was the daughter of Powhatan, chief of the Powhatan tribe, a branch of the Algonquians. According to *Smith's Generall Historie of Virginia, New England, and the Summer Isles* (1624), Jamestown

Pocahontas is credited with saving the life of Captain John Smith, a Jamestown colonist, in 1607.

colonist Captain John Smith was captured by the Powhatans in 1607 and held for execution. As the story goes, 12-year-old Pocahontas rescued Smith, thus saving the Jamestown colony from attack by the Powhatans. Historians now believe the sentencing of Smith to execution may have been staged and that the Powhatans never intended to kill him. Yet Pocahontas did play an important role in maintaining peaceful relations between the fragile Jamestown colony and the Powhatans. She brought much-needed food as well as information about her father's plans to the colonists.

After Smith returned to England, relations between Jamestown and the Powhatans began to deteriorate. Captain Samuel Argall had Pocahontas abducted and held captive in 1613. During her captivity, she converted to Christianity and married widower John Rolfe in 1614. The Virginia Company realized that Pocahontas (now called Rebecca) could be useful in promoting immigration and investment in the colony. In 1616 the company sent Pocahontas, John Rolfe, and their one-year-old son to England as an example of the peaceful relations between the Native Americans and the colonists. In England, she visited the queen and other important dignitaries. The following year she contracted a fatal illness and died. Relations between the Powhatans and the colonists disintegrated after the deaths of both Pocahontas and her father.

1608 ▪ Clara Peeters painted "still lifes"

Clara Peeters (1594–1657) was born in Antwerp, Belgium. (She is believed to have been married in Antwerp as well, although there is no record of the date or the name of her husband.) In 1608 Peeters began painting works that are now known as "still lifes"—arrangements of fruits, flowers, and dishes or other food vessels. She is most famous for "meal" still lifes that often depict fish. Peeters had a successful career of nearly half a century, during which she completed at least 32 signed works. Four of her paintings are displayed at the Prado Museum in Madrid, Spain, and others are in collections in Vienna, Austria, and the United States.

1608 ▪ Midwife Louise Bourgeois wrote text on childbirth

Frenchwoman Louise Bourgeois (1563–1636) was one of the first graduates of the Hôtel-Dieu, a school for midwives. (A midwife assists a woman in childbirth.) She became a noted authority on labor and delivery. In 1608 she published an illustrated book (a shortened form of the actual 14-word title is *Diverse Observations*) that explained the birthing process as well as the causes of miscarriage and premature birth. Widely used throughout Europe, the book was later translated into German and Dutch. Bourgeois was appointed midwife to Marie de' Medici, the queen of France, in 1610, by which time she had attended more than 2,000 births. She delivered the queen's first baby before an audience of 200 observers.

1609 ▪ Painter Judith Leyster was born

Judith Leyster (1609–1660) was born into a middle-class Dutch family. She received instruction in painting from established artists, including the Dutch master Franz Hals, and became well known for her genre scenes (scenes of everyday life). In 1636 she married Jan Miense Molenaer, a fellow painter. The couple, who had at least one son, enjoyed professional success in Amsterdam. During her career Leyster was the only woman member of the Haarlem painters' guild. After her death in 1660, the name of Judith Leyster was largely forgotten, and many of her works were said to have been painted by male artists such as Franz Hals. In the twentieth century feminist art historians worked to restore Leyster's rightful reputation.

1611 ▪ Mary Frith ruled London underworld

Mary Frith (1584–1659) was born the daughter of a shoemaker in London, England. At an early age she became attracted to life on the London streets. Frith began her criminal career by associating with pickpockets, dressing as a man so she could blend in with the male thieves who slipped in and out of crowded markets and fairs. Next she turned to highway robbery and earned the nickname Moll Cutpurse because she used a knife to cut travelers' belts, on which they carried purses. Also known as the Queen of Misrule, Frith became quite wealthy, and in her final years she ran a house of prostitution. Upon her death at the age of 75, she was buried face down according to her wishes.

1616 ▪ Artemisia Gentileschi joined Florentine Academy

Artemisia Gentileschi (c. 1593–c. 1652) was born in Rome, Italy, at the end of the sixteenth century. Her father, a well-known artist named Orazio Gentileschi, taught her to paint in his studio. In 1612 one of Gentileschi's instructors was found guilty of raping her. The scandalous trial served to blacken the young woman's reputation. Around the same time Gentileschi married and moved to Florence with her husband. Although the couple eventually separated, they had a daughter. By the time she was 23, Gentileschi was elected to the Florentine Academy, an unusual honor for a woman. Her dramatic paintings, often depicting biblical subjects, attracted wealthy clients. Considered the greatest of all Italian women artists, Gentileschi worked throughout Italy and in London, England.

1622 ▪ Mbande Nzinga founded African kingdom

Mbande Nzinga (1582–1663) was a royal princess in Ndongo, a kingdom that lay next to Portuguese West Africa (present-day Angola). She attempted to declare her kingdom independent of the Portuguese and free her people from the horrors of the slave trade. In 1622 she was sent to negotiate with the invading Portuguese by her brother, the king of Ndongo. While working for a peaceful settlement with the Portuguese, Nzinga converted to Christianity and was baptized Dona Aña de Souza. She ruled as Queen of Ndongo from 1624 but was driven out of the region by Portuguese troops around 1630. Nzinga then established a new kingdom, which she called

Matamba. She ruled with an iron hand as Queen of Matamba (1630–1663). Her kingdom thrived and enjoyed relative stability. According to some historical accounts, though, the new kingdom later assisted the Portuguese in their slave trade.

1622 ▪ Marie de Gournay published feminist work

Marie le Jars de Gournay (1565–1646) was the daughter of an influential Parisian court official who purchased her a feudal estate in Picardy. In 1580, after the death of her father, de Gournay lived in the castle with her widowed mother and siblings.

De Gournay was largely self-educated. When she was 18 she discovered the *Essays* of the French writer Michel de Montaigne. Moving back to Paris in 1588, she befriended Montaigne, who considered her an adopted daughter. She decided to remain single and to support herself and her family through her literary efforts.

Known as the French "Minerva" (meaning a woman of great wisdom or learning), de Gournay had financial success as a writer of treatises (written arguments that include an analysis of facts and reasoned conclusions) on various subjects. Her *Equality of Men and Women* (1622) and *Complaint of Ladies* (1626) demanded better education for women. She also edited the works of Montaigne after his death and became the hostess of a salon in Paris.

c. 1627 ▪ Maria Cunitz simplified Kepler's tables

Maria Cunitz (1610–1664) was a German scientist and the first female astronomer in Europe. She simplified the *Rudolphine Tables,* a statistical description of the motions of the planets published by the great German astronomer Johannes Kepler in 1627. Cunitz's work was acclaimed by scientists throughout seventeenth-century Europe.

1630 ▪ Qin Liangyu helped defeated Manchus

Qin Liangyu (1573–1648) was educated along with her brothers by their father at a time when women were not customarily educated in China. Qin married an aboriginal (native) chieftain named Ma Qiancheng, who was granted a title by the Ming state. Upon her husband's death, she inherited his title. In 1630 the Ming emperor summoned Qin to help defend the capital at Beijing against invading Manchu forces.

1632 ▪ Chinese poet Ye Ziaolan died

Ye Ziaolan (1616–1632) was the daughter of an elite family, and her literary aspirations were encouraged by both of her parents. When she died at the age of 16, she became a cult figure among south Chinese literary leaders who were as entranced by the story of her short life as by the beauty of her poetry.

1633 ▪ Louise de Marillac cofounded Sisters of Charity

Louise de Marillac (1591–1660) was born in Ferri Sres–en–Brie, France, and was orphaned by the age of fifteen. In 1613 she married Antoine Le Gras, with whom she had a son. After she was widowed in 1625, de Marillac turned to charitable works for the sick and poor under the direction of Roman Catholic priest Vincent de Paul. In 1633, starting in her Paris home, she and four young assistants founded the Sisters of Charity, who served in hospitals, orphanages, and schools. They began taking religious vows in 1642, but for only a year at a time. This practice continues in the Sisters of Charity today. Louise de Marillac was named a saint in 1934 and was declared the patron of Christian social work in 1960.

1634 ▪ Nur Jahan promoted learning and the arts

Nur Jahan (c. 1571–1645) was the empress of the Mughal (Mogul) empire. (The Mughals were a dynasty—or ruling family—of Muslims from Turkey who ruled India from 1526–1857.) During her reign Jahan promoted learning and the arts and entertained scholars, poets, architects, and painters. She also ordered the building of monuments and gardens in cities throughout the empire.

1637 ▪ Maria de Zayas y Sotomayor published feminist stories

Maria de Zayas y Sotomayor (1590–c. 1660) was born into a noble family in Madrid, Spain, but was brought up in Naples, Italy. Although she was an acclaimed poet, she is probably best known for her feminist short stories, which were widely read in her time. In these works, de Zayas criticizes the subjugation (being under the control of another; in this case, women being subjected to the authority of men) of women in Spanish society. The author wrote her stories in the picaresque tradition. (Picaresque stories feature the adventures of a rogue or a rascal—a mischievous person or a scoundrel.)

Little is known about de Zayas's life, although she probably lived in Zaragoza, Spain, because her novels were published there. In 1637 she published her first successful book, *Novelas amorosas y ejemplares* ("Exemplary and Amorous Novels"). Ten years later she wrote *Desenga'os amorosos, parte segunda del sarao y entertenimientos honestos* ("Disenchantments of Love, the Second Part of the Party and Entertainment"). De Zayas is considered one of the most important early feminists.

c. 1638 ▪ Puritan leaders banished Anne Marbury Hutchinson

Anne Marbury Hutchinson (1591–1643) was born in Lincolnshire, England, and moved with her husband, William Hutchinson, to Boston, Massachusetts. There she organized meetings in which she preached Antinomian (radical Puritan) views. Puritans were members of a sixteenth- and seventeenth-century Protestant group that broke away from the Church of England to pursue a stricter moral code and religious reform. Antinomians differed from Puritans by believing that God speaks directly to people, thus freeing them from having to obey church or civil laws.

Tried for heresy (violation of church doctrine) in 1638, Anne was banished from the colony along with her husband and their 11 children. They settled on the island of Aquidneck in Narragansett Bay. After William died in 1642, Anne and her children moved to a Dutch colony in an area that is now Pelham Bay in New York State. The following year Native Americans killed her and all but one of her family. Hutchinson was inducted into the National Women's Hall of Fame in 1994.

1638 ▪ Poet Sibylle Schwartz defended women writers

Sibylle Schwartz (Schwarzin) was born into an aristocratic family in Pomerania (an area in present–day Germany and Poland) and received a solid education. After her premature death from dysentery (an intestinal disease) at the age of 17, her poems were edited and published by writer Samuel Gerlach. Schwartz's poetry expresses her feelings of turmoil caused by the Thirty Years' War (1618–1648), which had driven her family from their estates. Gerlach called Schwartz the "Tenth Muse." (The Muses were nine sister goddesses in Greek mythology who presided over song, poetry, the arts, and the sciences.) She earned her name for her staunch defense of women writers, which prompted her to ask the particularly apt question, "Weren't the Muses women?"

c. 1639 ▪ Sister de l'Incarnation opened Ursuline convent

Marie Guyart (1599–1676) was born in Tours, France, and was widowed by the time she was twenty. Although religious visions prompted her to withdraw from the world, she worked in a family business for several years. But Guyart's visions continued, so in 1632 she left her son and entered the Ursuline cloister at Tours. She took her vows in 1633, becoming Sister de l'Incarnation. Six years later she moved to Canada and oversaw construction of the first Ursuline convent in Quebec.

While Sister de l'Incarnation governed the Ursulines, she also ran a boarding school for Native American and French girls, wrote several religious works in Native languages and in French, and composed over 12,000 letters. She was so firm in her views that the bishop of Quebec could not impose his authority over the Ursulines until after her death in 1676. (*Also see entry dated c. 1535: Angela Merici founded Company of St. Ursula.*)

1641 ▪ Writer Madelaine de Scudéry began career

Madelaine de Scudéry (1607–1701) moved to Paris, France, at a young age to join her brother, successful dramatist Georges de Scudéry, who was living there. She held a literary salon in her home, establishing herself as a successful hostess. In 1641 Madame de Scudéry began her literary career with the novel *Ibrahim ou l'illustre Bassa* ("Ibrahim; or, The Illustrious Bassa"). She continued to write lengthy novels about Paris society that became extremely popular because the characters were based on important figures, easily recognized by her readers. Treasuring her own independence by remaining single, she advocated the education of women both in her writing and in her salons. Although her works are no longer widely read, Madame de Scudéry had an impact on the development of the novel, particularly because of her masterful character analysis.

c. 1645 ▪ Deborah Moody received land grant

Deborah Moody (c. 1580–1659) was the first woman to receive a land grant in colonial America when she was given title to land in Kings County (now Brooklyn), New York. She was also the first colonial woman to vote.

c. 1645 ▪ Jewish memoirist Glückel of Hameln was born

Glückel of Hameln (c. 1645–1724) was born into a Jewish merchant family in the year 5407 of the Jewish calendar in Hamburg, Germany. Betrothed at 12 and wed at 14 to Chayim Hameln, she remained happily married until her husband's death in 1689. Glückel was then forced to take over the family business, pay off her husband's debts, and raise the eight of their 12 children who were not yet married. Since she was already an

"The London Midwives' Just Complaint"

In 1645 midwives (those who assist a woman in childbirth) in London published "The Midwives' Just Complaint." They called for an end to England's civil war (a rebellion against King Charles I that resulted in the establishment of a commonwealth, a type of political unit) so men could return home and women could start having babies again. The midwives asserted: "For many men, hopeful to have begot a race of soldiers, were there killed on a sudden, before they had performed anything to benefit midwives [meaning that these men died in battle before they could father children].... We were formerly well paid and highly respected in our parishes for our great skill and midnight industry; but now our art doth fail us."

advisor for her husband's business in gold and gems, she adapted quickly and managed to prosper. Her seven-volume memoir, published as *The Memoirs of Glückel of Hameln,* vividly describes the events of her life, family, and community up to 1719. It is considered the first work of modern Yiddish literature. (Yiddish is a German language written in Hebrew letters.)

c. 1648 ▪ Margaret Brent requested right to vote

Margaret Brent (c. 1601–c. 1658; some sources say 1671) was a lawyer and businesswoman who served as Lord Baltimore's attorney in the colony of Maryland. Credited with being the first woman lawyer in colonial America, Brent managed the family estate with her sister and handled her brother's legal affairs. Governor Leonard Calvert named Brent his executrix (the person responsible for settling his estate after his death). She was given the title "Lord" along with the power to sign contracts and conduct business—rights generally denied to women. In 1648 Brent claimed that, on the basis of her standing in the community, she deserved "a vote in the howse for herselfe and voyce allso." When the colonial assembly denied her request she demanded that all proceedings be declared invalid. At the time of her death, Brent owned thousands of acres of land in both Virginia and Maryland.

c. 1650 ▪ Anne Bradstreet's first poetry collection published

Anne Dudley (c. 1612–1672) was born in Northampton, England. In 1628 she married Simon Bradstreet, and two years later they immigrated with Puritans led by John Winthrop to the Massachusetts Bay Colony. (Puritans were members of a sixteenth- and seventeenth-century Protestant group that broke away from the Church of England to pursue a stricter moral code and religious reform.) While raising eight children, she wrote poetry. Without her knowledge, Bradstreet's brother-in-law John Woodbridge published her first collection, *The Tenth Muse Lately Sprung Up in America,* in London in 1650. Woodbridge assured readers in his preface that a woman wrote the poems and, moreover, that she did not neglect her family while doing so: "It is the work of a woman, honored, and esteemed where she lives, for her gracious demeanor, her eminent parts, her pious conversation, her courteous disposition, her exact diligence in her place, and discreet managing of her family occasions, and more than so, these poems are the fruit but of some few hours." Another edition of Bradstreet's poetry, *Several Poems Compiled with Great Variety of Wit and Learning,* was issued in 1678, six years after her death. She is considered the foremost poet of seventeenth-century North America.

1654 ▪ Queen Christina gave up throne

Christina (1626–1689) was the daughter of King Gustav II Adolf of Sweden. At the age of six she succeeded her father to the throne. She was educated while the kingdom was managed by Count Axel Oxenstierna, her father's chancellor (secretary). When she came of age in 1644 Christina attempted to end Sweden's involvement in the Thirty Years' War (1618–1648), which the country had entered in 1630 against the Holy Roman empire. More interested in patronizing the arts, Christina started Sweden's first newspaper, promoted literature and science, and supported industry. She refused to marry her cousin, who later became Charles X Gustav, instead naming him crown prince.

In the mid–1600s Christina also became interested in Roman Catholicism, which was prohibited in Sweden. In 1654 she shocked Europe by abdicating (giving up) the throne, going into self–imposed exile in Rome, Italy, and converting to Catholicism. Some historians believe she wanted to use her contacts as a way of positioning herself to become a candidate for the monarchy in Naples or in Poland. Failing to secure another throne, Christina spent the remainder of her life as a patron of the arts in Rome.

c. 1655 ▪ Verlinda Stone warned about Puritan threat

Verlinda (some sources spell given name "Virlinda") Graves Stone (c. 1615–1675) moved with her family to Maryland from Virginia in 1648. Her husband, Captain William Stone, had been appointed governor of Maryland. He invited Puritans—members of a sixteenth- and seventeenth-century

Protestant group that broke away from the Church of England to pursue a stricter moral code and religious reform—to join the colony, but they formed their own council (thus creating a rival government) in 1652. Three years later Captain Stone mounted an attack to dissolve the Puritan council. Miscalculating the Puritans' forces, he was wounded and taken prisoner. Verlinda Stone wrote to Lord Baltimore, the British supervisor of the colony, to inform him of the desperate situation. Her efforts were instrumental in restoring peace and religious tolerance in the region in 1657. After her husband's death in 1660, Stone continued to manage their large estate. When she died in 1675, she willed slaves, silver items, land, and pigs to her children—an unusual act for a woman at that time.

1656 ▪ Margaret Cavendish published her autobiography

Margaret Lucas (c. 1623–1673) was born into an aristocratic English family. At the age of 22 she married William Cavendish, the duke of Newcastle. During Puritan rule of England the couple lived in exile on the European continent because of their sympathies with the king. (The Puritans had broken away from the Church of England, which was headed by the king.) With the restoration of the monarchy in 1660, the Cavendishes returned to England. Margaret Cavendish pursued a literary career with great diligence, but her works were ignored. Indeed, her contemporaries called her "Mad Madge" on account of her eccentric behavior and dress. In all, she wrote 14 volumes, including scientific treatises (written arguments that include an analysis of facts and reasoned conclusions), poems, and plays. In recent years, feminists have studied her neglected writings for the light they shed on the situation of seventeenth-century women in England. Of particular interest is her autobiography, *The True Relation of My Birth, Breeding and Life* (1656).

c. 1658 ▪ Marguerite Bourgeoys advanced religion and education in Quebec

Marguerite Bourgeoys (d. 1700) was born in Troyes, France. In 1640 she joined a congregation of teachers attached to a convent in Montreal, Quebec. The convent was directed by the sister of Montreal governor Maisonneuve of Ville–Marie. Maisonneuve agreed to bring Bourgeoys to Montreal in 1653 if she would accept responsibility for educating the region's children.

Bourgeoys also devoted her early years in New France to resolving health problems among the area's people. With her subsequent advancement of educational and religious innovations, she became one of the most important figures in colonial life in New France. Despite the fact that Bourgeoys was revered as a saint when she died in 1700, she was not canonized until 1982.

1660 ▪ Mary Barrett Dyer executed for Quaker beliefs

Mary Barrett (c. 1610–1660) married William Dyer (or Dyre), a Puritan, in London in 1633. (Puritans were members of a sixteenth- and seventeenth-century Protestant group that broke away from the Church of England to pursue a stricter moral code and religious reform.) The following year the couple immigrated to the Massachusetts Bay Colony. Mary Dyer followed the teachings of Anne Hutchinson, who was banished from the colony in the late 1630s. Soon afterward colonial officials expelled Dyer, and the couple moved to Newport, Rhode Island, where they had five sons.

Later, after returning to England, Dyer was influenced by the teachings of George Fox, the founder of the Society of Friends (Quakers; members of a Christian sect that promotes justice, peace, and simplicity in living). When she went back to New England in 1657, the authorities arrested her under a new law forbidding Quakerism. She was released, however, when her husband (still a Puritan) promised to take her out of the colony. Mary and fellow Quakers William Robinson and Marmaduke Stephenson traveled back to Boston to challenge the

Native Women Helped Expand Fur Trade

From the earliest beginnings of the European fur trade in Canada, Native North American women were crucial to its functioning. European male fur traders found they could not survive in the Canadian bush without female companions who provided food, made clothing, and dressed the furs for trade. Through marriage to native women, European fur traders also made alliances with important trading families and were thus able to use existing trade networks to their own advantage.

outlawing of Quaker teachings. The court eventually sentenced all three to death by public hanging in 1660. (*Also see entry dated c. 1638: Puritan leaders banished Anne Marbury Hutchinson.*)

1662 ▪ Author Catharina Regina von Greiffenberg became famous

Catharina Regina von Greiffenberg (1633–1694) was born into the family of the barons of Seyssenegg in Lower Austria. Virtually self-educated, Catharina published *Geistlichen Sonette, Leider und Gedichte (Spiritual Sonnets, Songs, and Poems)* in 1662. Since women writers were not socially accepted at the time in Europe, many of the pieces in the collection were published earlier under male pen names. Because of the fear of Turkish invasions and the threat of persecution for the Protestant beliefs of her family, Catharina was forced to flee Austria for Nuremberg, Germany, in 1663. The next year she married her father's half-brother, and they returned to Austria to live until her husband's death in 1679. After that she spent the rest of her life in Nuremberg.

1664 ▪ Margaret Askew Fell imprisoned for preaching

Margaret Askew (1614–1702), was born in Lancashire, England. She married Thomas Fell, a prominent judge in Lancashire, and they had nine children. For a number of years beginning in 1651, the Fells allowed George Fox to use their home, Swarthmoor (Swarthmore), as the center for the Society of Friends, also known as the Quakers. This radical Protestant sect, organized by Fox, was based on the idea that humans are guided by their own "inner light" and do not need guidance from church leaders in the search for salvation.

Quakers gave women unusual freedom in religious life. Often called the "Mother of Quakerism," Margaret Fell helped the development of the Quaker movement by preaching, fund-raising, and letter-writing. Continuing her activities after her husband's death in 1658, she was imprisoned for four years, from 1664 to 1668. An impassioned advocate of the right of women to preach, she published *Women's Speaking Justified,*

Proved and Allowed of by the Scriptures in 1666. Three years later she married Fox.

c. 1665 ▪ Marie–Catherine Desjardins recognized as literary figure

Marie-Catherine Desjardins (1640–1683) was born into a poor family in the lower ranks of the French nobility. From 1655 on she made her home in Paris, where she supported herself as an author and gained recognition as a novelist, poet, and playwright. Writing 20 popular novels, Desjardins excelled in presenting her characters with psychological depth. The best known of her three plays was *The Favorite Minister* (1665), performed at the command of French king Louis XIV before his court at Versailles. Desjardins sometimes wrote under the pseudonym Madame de Villedieu. After a tragic love affair, she married Claude-Nicolas de Chastein in 1677 and bore him a son.

c. 1670 ▪ Writer Aphra Behn began career

Aphra Johnson Behn (1640–1689) was born near Canterbury, England, then spent several years in present-day Suriname (formerly Dutch Guiana, a republic in northern South America). In 1664 she married a Dutch merchant—his surname was Behn—in London, but she was widowed within three years. For a short time, Aphra Behn served as a paid spy for the English government in Antwerp, Belgium, during the Dutch Wars (1652–1654). Since she received no pay for this work, she fell into debt and was imprisoned. She then turned to writing as a profession. Behn's plays, numbering at least 14, were crude comedies that were highly successful in the 1670s. She also wrote witty poems and prose fiction. Her best-known novel, *Oroonoka* (1688), was based on her experiences in Suriname. Although Behn died in poverty in 1689, she was buried in Westminster Abbey, an honor reserved for the most respected British writers.

1670 ▪ Actress Marie Champmeslé debuted Racine roles

Marie Desmares (1642–1698) was probably born in Rouen, France. Taking her professional name from her second husband, actor Charles Chevillet Champmeslé, she was living in Paris by 1668. She became a popular actress as well as the mistress of famous playwright Jean Racine. Champmeslé debuted roles Racine wrote specifically for her, the best known being *Bérénice* (1670) and *Phèdre* (1677). When the Comédie Française troupe was formed in 1680, Champmeslé became its leading lady and continued to perform until she was forced to retire shortly before her death.

c. 1676 ▪ "Lily of the Mohawks" converted to Christianity

Kateri Tekakwitha (c. 1656–1680) was the daughter of a prominent Mohawk chieftain and a Christian woman who had been captured by the Algonquin. They lived in the Native American village of Ossernenon, New York. In 1660, when Tekakwitha was four years old, a smallpox epidemic killed both her parents and left her nearly blind. She was raised by her father's brother, the new chief, and his childless wife. Tekakwitha was baptized in 1676, taking the Christian name Kateri, or Katherine. Because she refused to marry and had converted to Christianity, she was harassed by other members of the tribe and eventually forced to flee to Sault Mission in Canada.

Tekakwitha became a mystic, engaging in severe penances that led to her premature death. Known as "the Saint" at Sault Mission and "Lily of the Mohawks" while still alive, she was named the "Protectress of Canada" among Christians in that country after her death. So many miracles were attributed to her that she came to be called the "Thaumaturge" or "Healer of the New World." Tekakwitha was beatified (declared a truly holy person and referred to thereafter as "Blessed") by the Roman Catholic church in 1980.

1676 ▪ Madame de Sévigné completed famous correspondence

Marie de Rabutin-Chanal (1626–1696), the daughter of a French baron, was orphaned at the age of six. Raised by her uncle, she was given a superior education. In 1644 she married Marquis Henri de Sévigné, who died seven years later. Madame de Sévigné thereafter devoted herself to raising her two children and pursuing literary interests in Paris. She is famous for the 1,700 letters she wrote to her married daughter between 1669 and 1676. In the letters she reported in a witty and conversational tone the events and gossip surrounding the court of Louis XIV, king of France. Madame de Sévigné's correspondence, published after her death, is said to have raised letter writing to the level of a fine art.

1677 ▪ Cockacoeske endorsed Treaty of Middle Plantation

Cockacoeske (?–1686) was the queen of the Pamunkey tribe of Native Americans. A leader of considerable influence and acumen, she worked for 30 years with the colonial government of Virginia to recapture the Pamunkey people's former political power. In the Treaty of Middle Plantation, the tribes pledged their allegiance to Cockacoeske as well as to the English king, Charles II. The king presented her with a silver badge and a scarlet robe, possibly for her assistance during Bacon's Rebellion (1676), an unsuccessful uprising against the aristocracy led by colonist Nathaniel Bacon that resulted in an end to Indian attacks. The Treaty of Middle Plantation ushered in a period of peaceful relations between the colonists and the Native Americans of Virginia's coastal plain. When Cockacoeske died in 1686, she was succeeded by her niece, Ann.

1678 ▪ Madame de Lafayette wrote *La Princesse de Clèves*

Marie-Madelaine Pioche de la Vergne, later known as Comtesse (countess) de Lafayette (1634–1693), was a member of the French aristocracy. In 1655 she married the Count de Lafayette, by whom she had two sons. In 1659, while her husband remained on his country estate, Madame de Lafayette began living independently in Paris. At her home she opened a famous literary salon (a meeting place set aside for intellectual conversation) and wrote several novels. Her masterpiece was *La Princesse de Clèves,* which was noted for its psychological insight into a heroine who struggled between her own desires and her duties. Although the novel was set in an earlier period, it reflected the manners and morals of the French court in the author's day. After the death of her longtime friend, the Duc de la Rochefoucauld, Madame de Lafayette spent the last decade of her life withdrawn from society.

1678 ▪ Elena Cornaro earned doctorate in philosophy

Elena Cornaro (1646–1684) was the daughter of a powerful Venetian (from Venice, a port city in northeastern Italy) family. In 1678, when she was 32 years old, she was awarded a doctorate in philosophy by the University of Padua in Italy. Cornaro was the first woman to achieve this distinction. She had carried out her studies privately, never attending the university. Refusing marriage to a wealthy man, she lived in association with a Benedictine convent as an adult.

1679 ▪ Painter-entomologist Maria Sibylla Merian published insect engravings

Maria Sibylla Merian (1647–1717) was born in Germany. A painter and entomologist (a zoologist who studies insects), she spent most of her life in Holland. In 1679 Merian began publishing *Erucarum Ortus,* a collection of engravings (drawings etched on a wood or metal plate and printed on paper) of the metamorphosis (changes during growth or development) of insects. In 1705 Merian's *Metamorphosis Insectroum Surinamensium* ("Metamorphosis of Insects of Surinam") appeared in Latin and Dutch. The book consisted of 60 plates engraved from watercolor paintings of insects that Merian had made while spending two years in the Dutch colony of Suriname in South America. Her work has been credited with helping to provide the basis for the classification of plant and animal species developed by eighteenth-century Swedish botanist Carolus Linnaeus.

1682 ▪ Mary Rowlandson wrote popular "Indian captive" narrative

Mary White Rowlandson (1636–1678) was a settler in Massachusetts Bay Colony. She and her two daughters and son were captured during King Philip's War (1675–1676), when tribal chief King Philip (Metacomet), a Native American chief of the Wampanoag people, attacked the colony. A week later

Rowlandson's youngest daughter died. Rowlandson and her surviving children were held in the custody of a warrior and his wife, who took them on a 12-week journey through the Connecticut River Valley. They were released when Rowlandson's husband paid a ransom. In 1682 Rowlandson wrote an account of the ordeal, *A True History of the Captivity and Restoration of Mrs. Mary Rowlandson*. The book was an immediate success, selling out four editions.

1682 ▪ Nell Gwyn helped establish hospital

Nell (Eleanor) Gwyn (1650–1687) was born in Hereford, England, to a poor family. While still in her teens she began working as an "orange girl" in London theaters, selling Spanish Seville oranges, which were then popular with audiences. By the age of 20 Gwyn was a comic actress known as "pretty, witty Nellie" and had particular success in "breeches parts," in which she wore trousers. In 1669 she became the mistress of King Charles II, with whom she had one son (and possibly a second). The only royal mistress who was liked by the people, Gwyn is credited with convincing the king to establish the Chelsea Hospital in London in 1682. That year she also made her last stage appearance. When Charles died in 1685, he reportedly said, "Let not poor Nelly starve." Gwyn herself died two years later.

1691 ▪ Sor Juana Inés de la Cruz wrote important feminist essay

Juana Inés de la Cruz (1648–1695) was born in San Miguel Nepantle, Mexico. At an early age she showed signs of great intelligence and was invited to live at the Mexican court by the wife of the viceroy (representative of the king of Spain). Finding life at court to be too frivolous (superficial, petty, or empty), Cruz briefly entered a Carmelite convent (an order of Roman Catholic nuns), returned to court, and finally took vows with the Hieronymite order in Mexico City. Noted for her beauty as well as her learning, Cruz later wrote that she became a nun because she had a "total lack of marital ambition"; she claimed she wanted to "live alone, in order to have no interruption to my freedom and my study."

Cruz continued her studies and wrote poetry and drama. During the Spanish Inquisition (a campaign by the Roman Catholic church to find and punish nonbelievers), a bishop told her to abandon learning because it was not a suitable pursuit for a woman. Cruz answered this charge with *Requesta* (1691; "Response")—now considered an important early feminist document—in which she claimed artistic heresy (violation of church doctrine) is not punishable by the pope. Choosing to devote her energies to caring for the poor, near the end of her life Cruz sold all of her books, scientific equipment, and musical instruments. She died of the plague (an infectious bacterial disease that strikes in epidemics, affecting large numbers of people) while fulfilling that mission.

1691 ▪ Luisa Roldán became sculptor for Spanish court

Luisa Roldán (c. 1656–1704) was born in Seville, Spain. Her father was the sculptor Pedro Roldán, who maintained a family workshop in which Luisa, one of her sisters, and two brothers were trained in the art of sculpting. Later her husband and son also joined the group, but it was Luisa who obtained royal commissions. Serving Spanish kings Charles II and Philip V, she created magnificent pieces in polychromed (decorated with several colors) wood and terra cotta (unglazed fired clay), a form she is credited with inventing.

c. 1694 ▪ Mary Astell called for improved female education

Mary Astell (1666–1731) was born into a middle-class English family. She never married, and she devoted most of her time to activities in female intellectual circles in London, England. Believing women were denied opportunities to develop their minds, she attempted to combat the stereotype that they were vain and frivolous creatures. Between 1694 and 1697 she published the two-volume work *Serious Proposal to the Ladies for the Advancement of Their True and Greatest Interest,* in which she called for the establishment of private institutions where single women could live together and receive a quality education. Although her proposal attracted

Manual for Women's Behavior Published

Published around 1700, the *Onna Daigaku* (name means "The Great Learning for Women") was a Confucian manual for ethics and the proper behavior of Japanese women. (Confucianism was a social philosophy originated by Chinese thinker Kong Fuzi, known as Confucius.) Although its authorship is uncertain, the manual is usually attributed to a male writer, Kaibara Ekiken (1630–1714). It is also thought that the work was based on earlier writings by Kaibara Token (1652–1713), the wife of the assumed author, who was herself a scholar. The text was a popular manual for the education of young women, particularly as they prepared for marriage. A specific code of behavior was prescribed: a woman was expected to be obedient and respectful at all times—to her parents as a daughter, to her husband and his family after marriage, and to her sons as a widow; her place was at home, and she was supposed to be diligent in her household labors. In eighteenth-century Japan a man could immediately divorce his wife for disobedience, jealousy, ill health, failure to produce a child, or even personal habits that he found offensive.

considerable interest among her contemporaries, it was not put into practice before her death in 1731.

c. 1698 ▪ Mademoiselle Maupin captivated audiences

Mademoiselle Maupin (first name unknown) (1670–1707) was the daughter of a secretary to the Count of Armagnac in France. She rose to fame as an opera singer in Paris, reaching her peak as a soprano between 1698 and 1705. Although she never had musical training, she compensated for this lack with her natural talent, charm, and beauty. Maupin was known for having many lovers, both male and female, and for her tempestuous (meaning sometimes violent) behavior, which included fighting duels with men. She left her husband, whom she married at a young age, but returned to him before her death in 1707. French writer Théophile Gautier based his novel *Mademoiselle Maupin, double amour,* on Maupin's colorful life.

1702 ▪ Anne became queen of England

Anne (1665–1714) was the daughter of King James II of England and his first wife, Anne Hyde. Although James was a Catholic, his daughter Anne was brought up as a staunch Protestant. In 1683 she married George, prince of Denmark. Of their 17 children, only one son, William, the Duke of Gloucester, survived infancy but he died at the age of twelve. Queen Anne ruled England from 1702 to 1714 after the deaths of her older sister Mary II and her brother-in-law William III. As queen she was totally dependent upon her ministers because of her chronic illnesses and her limited capabilities. Anne was the last Stuart ruler of England, having been succeeded upon her death by George I.

1703 ▪ Haiku poet Kaga no Chiyo was born

Kaga no Chiyo (1703–1775) was a famous author of haiku poems, a poetic form that originated in Japan and contains three lines with five, seven, and five syllables respectively. Chiyo's poems are collected in *Chiyo Ni kushu* and *Matsu no koe*.

1704 ▪ Maria Aurora von Königsmarck named provost of Quedlinburg Abbey

Maria Aurora von Königsmarck (1662–1728) was the daughter of a German nobleman who worked in Sweden. When her brother, Count Philipp Christoph Königsmarck, disappeared in 1694 (he was allegedly murdered), Maria went to Dresden, Germany, to search for him. While in Dresden she became the mistress of Frederick Augustus II "the Strong," prince of Saxony and future king of Poland. He was renowned both for his physical strength and his reputed 350 illegitimate children from many extramarital affairs. In 1696, a year before Augustus took the Polish throne, he and Maria had a son, Maurice of Saxony, who later became famous as a commander in the French army.

Noted for her refined ways, her love of culture, and her great beauty, Maria quickly rose through the ranks in the German courts because of her gift for languages and her musical talent. In 1702 King Augustus sent her to meet with Charles II of Sweden to arrange peace between Poland and Sweden. When the mission failed she fell out of favor with Augustus, who appointed her provost of the abbey at Quedlinburg (meaning she held the highest rank there) in 1704. Despite her obligations at Quedlinburg, she traveled extensively over the next 14 years and enjoyed court life until she retired to the abbey.

1708 ▪ Rachel Ruysch became court painter

Dutch artist Rachel Ruysch (1664–1750) was born in Haarlem, Holland, and studied with flower painter Willem von Aelst. At the age of 29 she married Juriaen Poole, a portrait painter, but she signed her works with her maiden name. In 1701 they were both admitted to the Hague Corporation of Painters. Seven years later they were invited to serve as court painters in Düsseldorf, Germany, making Ruysch the first woman to hold this appointment. They remained in Düsseldorf until the death of their patron, the elector (prince) of Palatine, in 1716, after which they returned to Amsterdam, Holland. Although Ruysch gave birth to ten children, she managed to have a successful artistic career. Noted for her detailed flower paintings, she continued to work until she died at the age of eighty-six. She enjoyed such a favorable reputation that she was able to give paintings as dowries (money or goods that a woman brings to her husband in marriage) for her daughters.

1714 ▪ Peasant poet He Shuangqing was born

He Shuangqing (1714–?) wrote poetry that was greatly admired by a circle of Chinese male literary leaders who collected and published her work. They valued the directness and the simplicity of her verses. She is reported to have sharpened her literary skills by listening to a maternal uncle, who was a village teacher.

1718 ▪ French dancer Marie Sallé made Paris debut

Marie Sallé (1707–1756), the daughter of an acrobat, was born in Paris, France. She became a child performer, appearing in pantomimes (stories dramatized silently, using only bodily and facial movements) in London and France and making her Paris debut at age eleven. After Sallé danced with the Paris Opera in 1727, she began performing widely on stage, playing the title role in *Pygmalion* (1733) and the part of Terpsicore in *Pastor fido* (1734), both by the British composer George Frideric Handel. She was especially popular in works by French composers Jean Philippe Rameau, Moliére, and Jean Baptiste Lully. Sallé was famous for her costuming innovations. For instance, when she danced in *Pygmalion* in London, she caused a sensation by wearing only a simple tunic in the style of a Greek statue instead of the elaborate skirts, bodices, and petticoats usually adopted by ballet dancers of her time. She also wore her hair loose, rejecting the customary head ornaments, and she moved her body freely. Sallé is thus known today as one of ballet's pioneers.

1718 ▪ Mary Wortley Montagu introduced smallpox vaccine

Mary Pierrepont Wortley Montagu (1689–1762), the daughter of the earl of Kingston, was born in London, England. She was primarily self-educated, learning Latin on her own and writing poetry at an early age. When she was 23 she eloped with Edward Wortley Montagu against her father's wishes. They lived in London, where Mary became popular for her wit and befriended such famous literary figures as Joseph Addison and Alexander Pope.

The Montagus moved to Constantinople (now Istanbul, Turkey) when Edward was appointed English ambassador in 1716. While there, Mary learned about smallpox inoculation. (Smallpox is a highly infectious viral disease characterized by skin eruptions, or "pox." It was carried to the Americas by Europeans, who spread it among Native Americans, killing untold numbers of people. A strict program of vaccination has since controlled the disease.) Upon returning to England in 1718, she introduced this new technique of disease prevention but encountered heated opposition from the medical profession.

During a smallpox epidemic in 1721, however, Montagu had her five-year-old daughter inoculated in the presence of doctors. The child suffered only a mild case of smallpox, which made her immune to the more deadly form of the disease. After the procedure was successfully tested on charity schoolchildren and convicts, King George even had his own grandchildren inoculated. Smallpox vaccination was then accepted by physicians, and many lives were saved.

c. 1720 ▪ Painter Rosalba Carriera introduced use of pastels

Rosalba Carriera (1675–1757), the daughter of a merchant, was born in Venice, Italy. Beginning her artistic career by creating designs for lace and decorating snuffboxes (a small box for holding pulverized tobacco), she turned to portrait painting while she was in her twenties. Carriera was the first artist to paint on ivory instead of vellum (fine-grained animal skin), but she is best known for introducing the use of pastels in portraiture. Consisting of paste made from powdered pigment, pastels allow the artist to paint quickly and produce subtle variations in color. Carriera's work became so popular that she received many commissions from royal patrons throughout Europe, including Louis XV of France and Augustus III of Poland. In 1720 she was elected to the French Academy of Painting and Sculpture, a rare honor for a woman. Carriera's sister Giovanna served as her assistant throughout the artist's career. Sadly, Carriera lost her sight during the last decade of her life.

1720 ▪ Pirate Anne Bonney captured and sentenced to death

One of the most sensational events in the annals of crime occurred with the capture of pirate Anne Bonney (some sources cite spelling of given name as "Ann"; some sources cite spelling of surname as "Bonny"). The illegitimate daughter of an Irish attorney, Bonney frequented the waterfront in Charleston, South Carolina, wearing men's clothing. In 1719 she eloped with James Bonney to the Bahamas, where she fell in love with a pirate named Calico Jack Rackham. He offered to buy a divorce from her husband, and when James Bonney refused, Anne and Rackham seized a ship. (Allegedly the crew members were ignorant of Anne Bonney's gender.)

Aboard the ship was another woman, Mary Read, who was disguised as a sailor. Bonney discovered Read's identity, and the two became a team. In November of 1720 Rackham's ship was captured, but Bonney and Read wounded several Royal Navy sailors during the battle. Both women were sentenced to hang. Asked whether the condemned had anything to say, Bonney and Read reportedly shouted, "Milord, we plead our bellies!"—both women were pregnant. Bonney is said to have delivered her baby and escaped, never to be seen again. (*Also see entry dated 1720: Sailor Mary Read convicted of piracy.*)

1720 ▪ Sailor Mary Read convicted of piracy

Mary Read was born in England and joined the Royal Navy when she was fourteen. During the War of the Spanish Succession (1701–1713; Britain, the Dutch, and Austria's Habsburgs v. France and Spain), she served her country with distinction. After the Peace of Utrecht, Read signed onto a Dutch ship known as a merchantman. When the vessel was captured by pirate Calico Jack Rackham, Read joined his crew. Anne Bonney, another female pirate and the partner of Rackham, soon discovered Read's identity, and the two became friends.

Upon falling in love with a crew member, Read revealed her gender. When her lover quarreled with a shipmate, the two men were sent ashore to settle their differences. Being an experienced swordswoman, Read insisted on taking her lover's place. After a fierce struggle, Read killed her opponent.

In 1720, when Rackham's ship was captured by the Royal Navy, the entire crew was sentenced to death. Read and Bonney, who were both pregnant, then revealed their identities to the court. Since British law forbids the execution of pregnant women, their sentences were commuted. Read died in childbirth in 1721. (*Also see entry dated 1720: Pirate Anne Bonney captured and sentenced to death.*)

1731 ▪ Giuseppa Eleanora Barbapiccola translated Descartes

Giuseppa Eleanora Barbapiccola translated noted French mathematician and philosopher René Descartes's *Principles of*

Philosophy into Italian. Nothing is known of her formal education, although she is reported to have been proficient in science and languages.

1732 ▪ Birth of Arakida Reijo

Japanese poet and novelist Arakida Reijo (1732–1806) became proficient in a variety of poetic styles, but the historical novels she later wrote were the works for which she is best known. These novels depict the lives of members of the Japanese aristocracy in the eleventh and fourteenth centuries.

c. 1736 ▪ Negotiator Molly Brant was born

Molly Brant was the sister of Mohawk chief Joseph Brant. Her Indian name was Konwatsi' tsiaienni, meaning "someone lends her a flower." Married to Sir William Johnston, a British agent, she was the leading matron of the Six Nations, a confederacy consisting of the Mohawk, Oneida, Onondaga, Cayuga, Seneca, and Tuscarawa tribes. Brant played an important role in negotiations during the American Revolution (the war for independence by the American colonies against the British government, 1775–1783). Giving assistance to the British Crown, she encouraged the Six Nations to keep its alliance with England when the war forced the Mohawk to relinquish their ancestral territories in New York State for a new home in upper Canada. Brant continued to work toward improving conditions of the Mohawk tribe's settlement throughout her life and remained a staunch loyalist to the Crown.

1738 ▪ Mathematician Maria Agnesi published first work

Maria Agnesi (1718–1799) lived with her family in Bologna, Italy, where her father was a professor of mathematics at the University of Bologna. The eldest of 21 children, she was a precocious child who assumed the responsibility of raising her brothers and sisters upon the death of her mother. Agnesi still had time for her studies, however, and by the age of 14 she had discussed philosophical questions with the learned men of Bologna.

When Agnesi was 20 she published *Propositions of Philosophy,* a collection of nearly 200 essays on a variety of subjects, such as philosophy, logic, elasticity, celestial mechanics, Newton's theory of gravitation, and the education of women. In this work Agnesi also solved an ancient mathematical puzzle with a formula (later known as "the witch of Agnesi") describing the curve that duplicates the volume of a cube. Ten years later she wrote *Analytical Institutions for the Use of Italian Youth,* in which she proposed new methods for studying algebra, geometry, and calculus. Establishing Agnesi's reputation as the most important woman scientist in Europe, the book was used as the standard mathematical text for 50 years.

In 1752 Agnesi was appointed honorary chair of mathematics at the University of Bologna, although she did not present lectures. Instead she established a hospital in her home; during the last 15 years of her life she was administrator of the Po Alberto Trivulzio Institution for the Care of the Elderly and Homeless.

1739 ▪ Eliza Lucas Pinckney developed indigo as crop

Eliza Lucas Pinckney (1722–1793) was born in Antigua, West Indies. In 1739 her family moved to South Carolina, where her father had inherited a plantation near present-day Charleston. From the age of 16 she helped her father manage the plantation. During this time she experimented with indigo, a crop that had previously proved impossible to grow in South Carolina. (The deep reddish-blue indigo plant is used to make blue dye.) In 1744 she married Charles Pinckney, and within three years her efforts at cultivating indigo were so successful that South Carolina planters were able to export 100,000 pounds of indigo dye to England. For approximately 30 years indigo trade bolstered the economy of South Carolina, until it declined during the Revolutionary War (1775–1783). After the death of her husband in 1758, Pinckney successfully managed their seven plantations in South Carolina. When she died in 1793 President George Washington was a pallbearer at her funeral.

1740 ▪ Maria Theresa became ruler of Habsburg empire

Maria Theresa, Archduchess of Austria (1717–1780), was born in Vienna, Austria. Her father, Emperor Charles VI (reigned 1711–1740), had no male heirs, so he convinced the European powers to agree to the Pragmatic Sanction, a treaty that guaranteed Maria Theresa inheritance of Habsburg territories in Central Europe. In 1736 she married Francis of Lorraine.

When her father died in 1740, Maria Theresa was only 23, pregnant with her second child, and completely unprepared for rule. Breaking the Pragmatic Sanction, King Frederick II of Prussia seized the province of Silesia, bringing on the War of the Austrian Succession (1740–48). Rising to the emergency, Maria Theresa rallied the support of her subjects and defeated the attacking Prussian armies. She ultimately gained the emperorship for her husband, who became Holy Roman Emperor Francis I. The territory of Silesia, however, remained with Prussia, despite her efforts to reclaim it in the Seven Years' War (1756–63).

During that time Maria Theresa instituted various reforms, revising the tax system, reorganizing the bureaucracy (the government's administrative policy-making group), establishing a more humane legal code, and initiating universal elementary education for both boys and girls. She maintained an active schedule, even while bearing 16 children, ten of whom survived. (The most famous—or infamous—later became Queen Marie Antoinette of France.) After the death of Francis I in 1765, Maria Theresa shared rule with her son and heir, Joseph II (1741–1790), until her death in 1780.

1740 ▪ Gabrielle-Emilie published a study of physics

Gabrielle-Emilie le Tonnelier de Breteuil, later Gabrielle-Emilie du Châtelet (1706–1749), was born to noble parents in Paris, France. At the age of 19 she married Comte du Châtelet-Lomont. She was, however, far more interested in study and philosophy than in marriage. A feminist before the word was invented, she wrote, "If I were king, I would give to women all the rights of humanity, especially those of the intellect."

Colonial Women Denied Equal Rights

During the colonial era in the United States, homes were like mini-factories in which women produced soap, candles, cloth, and food. If the woman who headed a household was not a good planner, her whole family suffered. In addition to attending to the family's health care needs, women delivered babies because male doctors considered it beneath their dignity to engage in such a practice.

Although women were crucial contributors to colonial society, they faced double standards. For example, while adulterous men generally received only fines, women were often put on trial and their names were published in the local newspaper. Colonial women were defined completely by their relationships to males: they were either daughters, sisters, wives, or someone's mother. After marriage, a woman's legal identity was merged with that of her husband. Even women's labor was considered inferior to men's work. Girls were hired out as servants, whereas boys became apprentices and received superior educations.

A great admirer of the French writer Voltaire, Madame du Châtelet became his mistress after they met in 1733. She provided Voltaire with financial support and a place to stay at her chateau at Cirey in France's Champagne region. They were inseparable for 15 years, traveling together and debating philosophy until her death in 1749. They set up a laboratory at the Cirey estate, studying fire, heat, and light. As a result of these experiments, Madame du Châtelet concluded that heat and light were types of motion. In 1740 she published her own scientific work, *Institutions de physique* (*Institutions of Physics*), and four years later she wrote *Dissertation sur la nature and propagation du feu* ("Essay on the Nature and Propagation of Fire"). She also produced the first French translation of *Philosophiae Naturalis Principia Mathematica,* a revolutionary study by British mathematician and physicist Isaac Newton. Published in 1759, ten years after Madame du Châtelet died, it is still considered the best French translation.

1741 ▪ Elizabeth Petrovna ascended to Russian throne

Elizabeth Petrovna (1709–1762), the daughter of Peter the Great and Catherine I of Russia, was born in Kolomeskoye, near Moscow. In 1741, at the age of 32, she assumed the Russian throne as a result of a conspiracy. Known primarily for her tyranny and immoral behavior, Elizabeth nonetheless encouraged the development of education and the arts. She founded both the University of Moscow (1755) and the Academy of Fine Arts in St. Petersburg (1758). Elizabeth supported Austria during the European wars of the mid-eighteenth century, enhancing Russia's position in international affairs. When she died in 1762, she was succeeded by her incompetent nephew, the grand duke Peter. Within six months, however, the throne was seized by the bride whom Elizabeth had selected for Peter: Catherine the Great. (*Also see entry dated 1762: Catherine the Great became empress of Russia.*)

1745 ▪ Madame du Pompadour was the mistress of Louis XV

Madame du Pompadour (1721–1764) was born Jeanne Antoinette Poisson in Paris, France. When she was young her father, a financier, fled the country and left her in the care of Le Normant de Tournehem. Although she married Tournehem's nephew, Le Normant d'Etoiles, in 1741, she did not conceal her ambition to be the mistress of the king of France. Noted for her sense of style, Poisson set fashion trends. By 1745 the beautiful and talented Poisson had indeed caught the eye of King Louis XV, who called her "the most delicious woman in France." After the death of his previous mistress and Poisson's separation from her husband, the two became lovers. The king named her the Marquise de Pompadour—making her a noblewoman—and gave her a private apartment at Versailles, his palace. As Louis's official mistress, Madame Pompadour enlivened the court with balls and banquets. She was also a patron of the arts, supporting painters and architects and befriending such writers as Voltaire. Pompadour's immense power over the king allowed her to control military and government policies, creating hostility among members of the nobility, who despised her for her common birth. In fact,

Madame Pompadour was the virtual ruler of France for almost 20 years until her death at Versailles in 1764.

1757 ▪ Botanist Jane Colden cataloged plants

Jane Colden (1722–1764) was the daughter of Caswallader Colden, who served as royal acting governor in the New York colony. She was married to a man named William Farquar. Trained in botany by her father, Colden had catalogued and illustrated more than 300 specimens of plants in the New York region by 1757. She did not label the plants with their Latin names, however, because her father did not teach her the language, thinking women were incapable of learning it. In 1770, six years after Colden died in childbirth, the British Royal Society published a description of a gardenia species and attributed its discovery to naturalist Alexander Garden; actually, Colden had discovered and named the plant.

1760 ▪ Italian anatomist Anna Morandi gained fame

Anna Morandi (1716–1774) was born in Bologna, Italy. In 1780 she married Giovanni Manzolini, a professor of anatomy (the study of the human body) at the University of Bologna. They had six children. Under Manzolini's instruction, Morandi became proficient in making wax models of the human body, which he used in his lectures. When Manzolini fell ill, Morandi delivered his anatomy lectures for him, and after his death in 1760 she was appointed to his position at the university. As a professor of anatomy, Morandi received invitations to lecture in several foreign countries, and her wax models were widely used in teaching institutions throughout Europe.

1761 ▪ Hester Needham Bateman registered her own hallmark

Englishwoman Hester Needham Bateman (1709–1794) worked as a silversmith with her husband, John Bateman, until his death in 1760. She then managed their business herself, and in 1761 registered her own hallmark (engraved stamp)—"H.B."—becoming the first woman to do so. Bateman is now regarded as one of the great eighteenth-century silversmiths.

1762 ▪ Catherine the Great became empress of Russia

Catherine (1729–1796) was born in Stettin, Germany (now Poland), as Sophia Friederica Augusta, princess of Anhalt-Zerbst. In 1745 she went to Russia at the invitation of Empress Elizabeth Petrovna to marry the grand duke Peter, the heir to the throne. The young German princess took the name "Catherine" for her royal role. The couple had a son, who later became Emperor Paul I. But Catherine and Peter's marriage was a failure; Catherine had affairs with Gregory Orlov and Stanislaw Augustus Poniatowski. In 1762 her husband took the throne as Peter III, but within six months Catherine replaced him, becoming the sole Russian monarch through a palace revolution. Soon afterward Peter was murdered by Orlov and others.

Known as "Catherine the Great," the empress increased the power and domination of Russia during her reign. Among her achievements were the reform of local government and the extension of Russian territory to the Black Sea and into Poland. A well-educated woman, Catherine corresponded with some of the most distinguished intellectuals of the day, including French thinkers Voltaire and Deterre. In 1764 she opened the Smolny Institute—a secondary school for girls of noble birth—in St. Petersburg, thus demonstrating her concern for better education of Russian women.

Catherine the Great became sole ruler of Russia after a palace revolution in 1762.

1763 ▪ Catherine Sawbridge Macaulay published history

Catherine Sawbridge (1731–c. 1796) was born in Wye, Kent, England, and was educated by her father, who taught her Latin and Greek. In 1760 she married Scottish physician George Macaulay, who died six years later. In 1763 she began publishing *History of England from the Accession of James I to That of the Brunswick Line,* an eight-volume work that was completed in 1783. Although the study was immensely popular, many found it controversial because of Macaulay's radical republican sympathies. (She favored a form of government headed by a president, not a monarch.) In 1778 Macaulay married William Graham, who was nearly half her age. Among her last books was *Letters on Education* (1787), an appeal for better education for women.

1765 ▪ Angelica Kauffmann joined Royal Academy of Art

Angelica Kauffmann (1741–1807), the daughter of a traveling Austrian artist, was born in Chur in present-day Switzerland. Deciding to become an artist herself, she moved with her family to Italy and by age 11 she was painting portraits of prominent Italians. Her father managed her business affairs. In 1762 she was admitted to the Florentine Academy. Four years later she settled in London, England, where she befriended the great British portraitist Joshua Reynolds. Imitating Reynolds's style, Kauffmann continued her portrait work—she painted a portrait of Reynolds himself in 1769—and also began painting classical and mythological subjects. She was secretly married in 1767 to an adventurer named Count Van Horn, who was exposed as a bigamist (a person who has more than one spouse), leading to Kauffmann's public humiliation. In 1769 she was nominated to the newly formed Royal Academy of Art, becoming one of the founding members. Kauffmann is best known for decorative wall paintings she executed in the 1770s. After 1781 she married Venetian painter Antonio Zucchi and returned with him to Italy. She earned a reputation as one of the most successful and famous artists in her adopted city of Rome.

1768 ▪ Madame du Barry became mistress of King Louis XV

Madame du Barry was born Marie Jeanne Bécu (1743–1794) in the village of Vaucouleurs, France. She was the illegitimate daughter of a peasant woman and a Catholic monk. Bécu moved to Paris as a child, spending eight years in a convent and then working several years as a salesperson in an exclusive shop. Her beauty was legendary among Parisian noblemen, who called her "the Angel." One of them was Count Jean du Barry, who made her his mistress and trained her to be a courtesan (a prostitute with wealthy clients). He introduced her at court as "Mademoiselle Lange." In 1768 she attracted the attention of King Louis XV, who arranged for her to marry court attendant Count Guillaume du Barry, her lover's brother, so that she could qualify to be the king's official mistress. She succeeded Madame du Pompadour, the previous royal mistress, who had died four years earlier.

Within two years Madame du Barry had gained considerable power at court, but she was unpopular with the public because of her extravagance. Although she generously supported the arts, she was banned from court when the king died in 1774. During the French Revolution, a movement to overthrow the French aristocracy that began in 1789, du Barry was put on trial for having wasted the state's money. She was beheaded on the guillotine in 1794. (*Also see entry dated 1745: Madame du Pompadour was mistress of Louis XV.*)

Madame du Barry's extravagant tastes and love of power led to her beheading 1794.

1769 ▪ Elizabeth Montagu wrote about Shakespeare

Elizabeth Robinson (1720–1800) was born in York, England. In 1744 she married Charles Montagu, a wealthy aristocrat. Known as the "Queen of the Bluestockings" (intellectual women), Elizabeth established a literary salon at her townhouse. It soon became the center of intellectual society in London during the mid-eighteenth century, attracting such notable figures as actor David Garrick, painter Joshua Reynolds, and dramatist Hannah More. Also a noted literary critic, Montagu published one of her more important works, *Essay on the Writings and Genius of Shakespeare,* in 1769. Upon her husband's death, she turned her interests to architectural projects, building Montagu House. It still stands in London, at 22 Portman Square.

c. 1770 ▪ Elizabeth Chudleigh opened brandy distillery

Although Englishwoman Elizabeth Chudleigh (1720–1788) was illiterate, her beauty and charm allowed her to enjoy favor at court. She had love affairs with several noblemen before secretly marrying John Hervey, the brother of the second earl of Bristol, in 1744. She then separated from Hervey and denied her marriage to him under oath so she could marry the second duke of Kingston in 1769. When the duke died four years later she was charged with bigamy by his nephew. Found guilty in 1776, she had her marriage to Hervey, now the third duke of Bristol, declared valid.

Because she had caused a scandal in England, Chudleigh spent most of her life on the European continent. In the late 1770s she became a favorite in the court of Catherine II in Russia. During that time Chudleigh opened a brandy distillery in the Russian city of St. Petersburg. She was the model for the characters Beatrix Esmond in *The History of Henry Esmond* (1852) and Baroness Bernstein in *The Virginians* (1857–1859), both novels by British writer William Makepeace Thackeray. (*Also see entry dated 1762: Catherine the Great became empress of Russia.*)

c. 1771 ▪ Christiana Campbell ran popular tavern

Christiana Burdett Campbell (1722–1792) was the daughter of John Burdett, a tavernkeeper in Williamsburg, Virginia. The widow of an apothecary (druggist), Campbell ran a popular tavern behind the capitol building in Williamsburg. According to the *Virginia Gazette,* Campbell's tavern offered lodging, gambling, and food to patrons. During the 1760s and 1770s George Washington was a frequent visitor to Campbell's establishment, where "genteel Accommodations" and the "very best Entertainment" were available. Business declined when the state capital moved to Richmond in 1780. Campbell—remembered by a Yorktown merchant as "a little old Woman about four feet high; & equally thick"—closed her business by 1783.

1771 ▪ Catherine Kaidyee Blaikley delivered 3,000 babies

Catherine Kaidyee Blaikley (1695–1771) was a midwife (a woman who assists in childbirth) in Williamsburg, Virginia.

Her death notice in 1771 stated that during her career she had delivered "upwards of three Thousand Children."

1774 ▪ Marie Antoinette became queen of France

Marie Antoinette (1755–1793) was born in Vienna, Austria, the daughter of Holy Roman Emperor Francis I and Empress Maria Theresa. In 1770, when she was just 14, she married the heir to the French throne, who became King Louis XVI four years later. As a young, inexperienced queen, Marie was unpopular with the French people, who viewed her as a foreigner. They considered her to be arrogant (overly proud and full of self-importance), promiscuous (engaging in casual sex with many different partners), and a bad influence on the king. She was therefore surrounded by scandal and rumors about her disloyalty to France.

When the French Revolution (1789–1799) broke out in 1789, Marie Antoinette was the target of much hatred and was accused of favoritism to her native Austria. (The French Revolution was a movement to overthrow the monarchy and replace it with a democratic form of government.) Throughout the period of constitutional monarchy (1789–1791), during which the king ruled according to a constitution, she urged her husband to resist the revolutionaries. As the revolution progressed, however, it became clear that the monarchy would fall. On the night of June 20, 1791, Louis XVI and Marie Antoinette attempted to flee the country, but they were recognized and captured. The king was executed on the guillotine on January 21, 1793. Marie Antoinette remained a prisoner until October 16, 1793, when she went to the guillotine as well. She died with grace and simple dignity, winning over many of her former enemies. Still, she remains a notorious and unpopular figure in French history. (*Also see entry dated 1740: Maria Theresa became ruler of Habsburg empire.*)

1774 ▪ Clementina Rind published *Virginia Gazette*

Clementina Rind (1740–1774) was the wife of the public printer in Williamsburg, Virginia. Upon her husband's death in 1774 the Virginia House of Burgesses appointed Rind in his place. Taking control of her husband's printing business, she assumed publication of his newspaper, the *Virginia Gazette*. The paper included foreign, domestic, and shipping news, as well as essays, poems, and advertisements, in accordance with the *Gazette*'s motto: "Open to ALL PARTIES, but Influenced by NONE." Rind became the most famous woman of affairs in eighteenth-century Virginia.

1775 ▪ Mary Katherine Goddard printed the Declaration of Independence

Mary Katherine Goddard (1738–1816) was born in Connecticut and was educated at home. After her father's death in 1762 she moved to Providence, Rhode Island, where her brother William printed the *Providence Gazette*. Relocating to Philadelphia, Pennsylvania, in 1765, they published the *Pennsylvania Chronicle* for five years before heading to Baltimore, Maryland, to publish the *Maryland Journal*. Mary took over the newspaper in 1775. That same year the Continental Congress, which had moved to Baltimore from Philadelphia, commissioned her to print the first official copies of the Declaration of Independence. Operating the printing presses herself, Goddard paid post riders to deliver the freshly printed Declaration throughout the colonies. She left the printing business in 1784 after she and her brother reportedly quarreled. In addition to running a bookshop until 1810, Goddard was also the postmaster of Baltimore from 1775 until 1779.

1776 ▪ Laura Bassi became university professor

Laura Bassi (1711–1778), the daughter of a well-to-do lawyer, was born in Bologna, Italy. Receiving an excellent education as a child, she was awarded a philosophy degree from the University of Bologna in 1732. That same year she was named a university lecturer in universal philosophy, as well as a member of the prestigious Academy of Sciences in Bologna. In 1738 Bassi married one of her colleagues, Guiseppe Veratti. The couple had 12 children. In 1776, at the age of 65, Bassi was appointed professor of experimental physics (the science that deals with matter and energy) at the

Female Army Nurses and Matrons Went to War

In 1775 the U.S. Second Continental Congress authorized a medical department and established three hospitals for the new army of 20,000 soldiers. Each hospital was composed of a medical staff that would follow the army and include a director, chief physician, four surgeons, an apothecary (druggist), 20 surgeon's mates, a clerk, two storekeepers, a nurse for every ten patients, and a nurse matron (to supervise the nurses and oversee the wards) for every 100 patients.

General George Washington specifically requested female nurses and matrons so that men could be freed for battle. A nurse was authorized one-fifteenth of a dollar per day in pay, or two dollars per month, plus a daily food ration. A matron received one-half of a dollar per day, or 15 dollars per month, and a daily food ration. By the end of the war a nurse's pay had quadrupled to eight dollars per month but was still unbelievably low, equaling the amount a senior surgeon would make in just two days.

University of Bologna. A pioneer female physicist, Bassi was also unique during her time as a woman teacher of male students at the university level. Throughout her long career she was an active educator and researcher in the field of physics. Her studies on electricity are particularly noteworthy.

1776 ▪ Molly Corbin took husband's place in battle

Margaret "Molly" Corbin (1751–1800) was born in Franklin County, Pennsylvania. From the age of five she was raised by a relative because her father had been killed in a battle with Native Americans and her mother had been taken prisoner. In 1776 Corbin's husband enlisted in the American Revolution (1775–1783; a movement by American colonists for freedom from Britain), and she accompanied him to help look after the soldiers. During a battle at Fort Washington, New York, she stood alongside her husband as he fought. When he was mortally (fatally) wounded she immediately took his place, without hesitation reloading his cannon and taking responsibility for his battle station.

Suffering permanent disability due to the loss of one arm, Corbin began a series of appeals to the government for financial assistance. In 1779 the Supreme Council of Pennsylvania awarded her a 30-dollar grant, and Congress approved a military pension, including all military benefits given to a Revolutionary War veteran. Corbin also registered with the Invalid Regiment, created in 1777 for those wounded in service. She remained with the Invalid Regiment until it was disbanded in 1783.

1776 ▪ Ann Lee established Shaker community

Ann Lee (1736–1784) was born in Manchester, England, the daughter of a blacksmith. In 1758 she joined the "Shakers," a radical group of Quakers. (The Shakers were so named because they danced with shaking movements during religious worship.) Four years later Lee was forced to marry Abraham Stanley, a blacksmith, against her will. After all four of their children died in early childhood she persuaded her husband to become a Shaker. Lee soon developed a reputation for street preaching, for which she was imprisoned in 1770. While in prison she said she had a vision, which revealed that Christians should remain celibate (refrain from sexual intercourse) in order to do Christ's work. Escaping persecution, Lee and a band of followers immigrated to the United States in 1774. Two years later Lee established a Shaker community at Niskayuna (now Watervliet), New York. Known as "Mother Lee," she became the leader of the group and stipulated that men and women must live separately.

c. 1776 ▪ Betsy Ross made first American flag

Elizabeth "Betsy" Ross (1752–1836) was born in Philadelphia, Pennsylvania. She was the daughter of Samuel Griscom, a builder who constructed a large part of Independence Hall in Philadelphia. In 1773 she married John Ross, a successful upholsterer and flagmaker. After his death in 1776 she established a flagmaking business. According to folk history, she was approached by George Washington, Colonel George Ross, and Robert Morris, all members of a secret committee from the Continental Congress. They are said to have asked Ross to make the first American flag, the "Stars and Stripes." Although this story has long been told to schoolchildren, its truth remains questionable.

1777 ▪ Mary Willing Byrd managed plantation

Mary Willing (1740–1814) was born in Philadelphia, Pennsylvania. In 1761 she wed William Byrd III of Virginia, eventually bearing ten children during 16 years of marriage. After her husband went bankrupt and committed suicide in 1777, Byrd faced the task of settling his estate, satisfying numerous creditors, and preserving an inheritance for her children. She took over management of Westover, their Charles County plantation in Virginia. Byrd's financial difficulties occurred in the midst of the American Revolution (1775–1783), a war for independence by the American colonies against the British government. At one point she was even accused of being a spy for the British. Because British troops landed three times at Westover, revolutionary leaders suspected Byrd of having Loyalist (pro-British) sympathies and engaging in illegal commerce. Byrd survived the war, however, without being brought to trial. Upon her death in 1814 she was able to provide financially for her children and grandchildren.

c. 1778 ▪ Hannah Lee Corbin proposed suffrage

Hannah Lee Corbin (1728–1782) was born in Westmoreland County, Virginia. An unconventional woman, she became a Baptist in the 1760s, despite the fact that the Anglican religion was the accepted religious sect at that time and Baptists were considered a dissenting (nonconformist; going against established and accepted tradition) group. When Corbin was widowed at age 32, she preserved her children's inheritance by apparently living with (but not marrying) Dr. Richard Lingan Hall, with whom she had two additional children. Corbin's brother, General Richard Henry "Lighthorse Harry" Lee, was a leader of the Virginia delegation to the Continental Congress.

Corbin complained to him that she was a victim of taxation without representation and, as a propertied widow, should have the vote. Lee reminded her that Virginia women already had the right to vote.

1779 ▪ Store owner Ann Neill marketed toothpaste

Ann Neill announced the opening of her general store in the *Virginia Gazette*. She sold small household wares, musical instruments, ladies' hats, pocket pistols, liquor, groceries, and other assorted items. By 1779 Neill was also selling her own brand of dentifrice (toothpaste).

1779 ▪ Elisabeth Vigée-Lebrun gained fame as a portraitist

Elisabeth Vigée-Lebrun (1755–1842) was born Marie Anne Elisabeth Vigée in Paris, France, the daughter of a painter. In 1776 she married J. B. P. Lebrun, an art dealer and grandnephew of French painter Charles le Brun (surname sometimes cited as "Lebrun"). Vigée-Lebrun soon gained her own reputation as a painter of portraits. Her excellent sense of color and her ability to paint flattering yet believable likenesses of her subjects made her a favorite artist of the French royal court and nobility. Vigée-Lebrun executed memorable portraits of Queen Marie Antoinette and Madame du Barry, official mistress of Louis XV. At the start of the French Revolution (1789–1799; a movement to replace the French monarchy with a democratic form of government) she left Paris for Italy. Traveling throughout Europe, Vigée-Lebrun achieved great success, producing portraits of many of the era's most prominent women, including author Germaine de Staël. In London in the early 1800s she painted the Prince of Wales, English poet Lord Byron, and other well-known figures. She returned to Paris in 1805. (*Also see entry dated 1768: Madame du Barry became mistress of King Louis XV; and 1774: Marie Antoinette became queen of France.*)

1782 ▪ Deborah Sampson joined colonial army

Deborah Sampson (1760–1827) was born in Plympton, Massachusetts. She was a schoolteacher before joining the

Continental Army at the age of 21 during the American Revolution (1775–1783, a war for independence by American colonies against the British government). Dressed in men's clothing, Sampson joined a company of volunteers under the name Robert Surtlieff and served for 18 months. After being wounded twice and suffering from "brain fever," she was taken out of action. Her true identity was then discovered, and she was discharged in 1783. Returning to her home in Massachusetts, she married Benjamin Gannett and together they raised three children. Gannett's biography, written by Herman Mann and titled *The Female Review,* was published in 1797.

1782 ▪ Princess Ekaterina Dashkova encouraged Russian culture

Ekaterina Romanovna Vorontsova (1744–1810) was born in St. Petersburg, Russia. In 1759 she married Prince Mikhail Dashkov, but he died three years later. Dashkova was a close confidante of Empress Catherine II, also known as Catherine the Great. In 1782 the empress appointed her director of the St. Petersburg Academy of Arts and Sciences. Holding this position from 1783 until 1796, Dashkova encouraged the development of Russian language and literature. She was instrumental in establishing the Russian Academy to promote the study and use of the Russian language. As the first president of this institution, she directed the publication of a Russian dictionary. A writer and editor herself, Dashkova was a prominent patron of literature until Catherine's death in 1796. Forced to leave St. Petersburg by Catherine's successor, Emperor Paul I, Dashkova lost her position of influence. (*Also see entry dated 1762: Catherine the Great became empress of Russia.*)

1784 ▪ Hannah Adams published religious survey

Hannah Adams (1755–1831) was born in Medfield, Massachusetts. She is considered the first American woman to support herself as a professional writer. In 1784 Adams published her first important book, *The Alphabetical Compendium of the Various Sects,* a historical survey of religions. She also wrote *A Summary History of New England* (1799) and *The*

History of the Jews (1812). Adams' autobiography, which was published in 1832, after her death, provides a valuable history of colonial America.

1786 ▪ Astronomer Caroline Herschel discovered comets

Caroline Herschel (1750–1848) was born in Hanover, Germany. In 1772 she joined her brother William in London, England, to assist him in his work as a musician. Within ten years William had abandoned music to become an astronomer (one who studies the matter that exists outside Earth's atmosphere). Collaborating with him in that pursuit as well, Caroline went on to make significant contributions to the field of astronomy. Between 1786 to 1797 she discovered eight comets and the Andromeda nebula. (Nebulae—plural for nebula—are clouds of gas or dust in space.)

In 1787 Herschel became William's professional assistant, earning a salary of 50 pounds a year from the British king. She published the *Index to Flamsteed's Observations of the Fixed Stars* in 1798. After her brother's death in 1822 she returned to Hanover and edited his catalog of nebulae. Six years later she was honored with a Gold Medal of the Royal Astronomical Society. Elected an honorary member of the Royal Astronomical Society in 1835, Herschel became a full member of the Irish Academy in 1838. The king of Prussia commemorated her ninety-sixth birthday by awarding her a gold medal.

1789 ▪ Charlotte Brooke published *Reliques of Irish Poetry*

Charlotte Brooke (1740–1793) was born in Rantavan, County Cavan, Ireland. She was among the youngest of 22 children of well-known writer and playwright Henry Brooke and Lettice Digby Brooke. Brought up in a literary household, Brooke devoted her life to her widowed father until his death in 1783, when she herself turned to writing. Using her knowledge of the Irish language, which she had learned as a child (probably from workers on her family estate), she published *Reliques of Irish Poetry* (1789), translations of Irish songs, odes (poems of praise), elegies (tributes to the dead), and lyrics.

Now considered the first work of Irish scholarship, Brooke's book was an important contribution to the revival of Irish-language literature, which had been suppressed since British occupation of Ireland in the seventeenth century. In spite of this achievement, however, Brooke lived in near-poverty after her father died. Hoping to earn a decent income, she applied for the position of housekeeper at the newly formed Irish Academy, but the trustees—who were her colleagues—determined that such a job would be beneath her social level. Brooke's application for membership in the academy was also denied because she was a woman. She spent her final days subsisting on financial gifts from friends. In addition to *Reliques,* Brooke wrote *School for Christians* (1791) and *Account of Henry Brooke* (1792), a biography of her father, which was published a year before her death.

1791 ▪ Olympe de Gouges declared rights of women

Olympe de Gouges (1748–1793) was born Olympe Gouze to a poor family in Montauban, France. Upon the death of her husband in 1789 she moved to Paris, where she became an actress and took the more noble-sounding name Olympe de Gouges. She also began her involvement in the French Revolution (1789–1799), a movement to overthrow the French aristocracy and establish a republic. Gouges was outraged that the revolutionary government had drafted the *Declaration of the Rights of Man and of the Citizen,* which guaranteed basic civil liberties to men but totally neglected women's rights. In response, she wrote *The Declaration of the Rights of Woman*

The Women's March on Versailles

During the so-called October Days of October 5–7, 1789, the French Revolution (1789–1799) gained new momentum as a result of the actions of a crowd of poor Parisian street women. A demonstration by female street vendors became the Women's March on Versailles as poor women in need of food gathered and marched on the royal palace at Versailles, 20 miles away. The armed women murdered the palace guards and seized the royal family (King Louis XVI and Queen Marie Antoinette), dragging them back to Paris. The Women's March on Versailles, which took place without male leadership, marked a crucial turning point in the French Revolution by making the king vulnerable to the will of the people.

and Citizen, a 17-point document that demanded recognition of women as political, civil, and legal equals of men.

In 1792 Gouges angered revolutionaries by criticizing their leaders, Jean Paul Marat and Maximilien-François Robespierre, and asking that the king's life be spared. She sealed her fate when she circulated a flyer stating that the type of government for the new French Republic should be determined by the people at large, not just the rebel leaders. Gouges was found guilty of undermining the Republic and beheaded on the guillotine in 1793.

1792 ▪ Théroigne de Méricourt championed women's rights

Théroigne Anne Josephe Théroigne (1762–1817) was born in Marcourt, Belgium. She later adopted the name of her village in the form of "de Méricourt." Attending a convent school only briefly, she worked during her early years as a farmworker, dressmaker, and governess. Méricourt studied singing in London, England, before moving to Paris, France, in 1785. During the early stages of the French Revolution (1789–1799; a movement advocating the overthrow of the monarchy and the establishment of a democratic form of government), she became a member of the Fraternal Society of Patriots of Both Sexes and participated in the Women's March on Versailles. She also cofounded a short-lived society called *Club des amies de la loi* (Society of the Friends of Law), which was dedicated to informing people about their rights. In 1790 she went to Belgium, where she was arrested for inciting revolution and sent to an Austrian prison.

After her release in 1791, Méricourt returned to Paris and was greeted with honor and acclaim. In a speech before the Fraternal Society, she advocated the formation of a women's battalion (army), "a company of Amazons," but she failed to attract middle-class women to this cause. In 1792 she took part in the attack on the Tuileries, the royal palace in Paris. Once honored for her heroism, Méricourt was later denounced by the Jacobins (a radical French revolutionary group), who called her a "She-devil in ruffles." In 1793 she sided with the Girondists (a more moderate group of French revolutionaries) in their split with the Jacobins and was then flogged (beaten) nearly to death. Méricourt went insane and died in a French asylum in 1817.

1792 ▪ Mary Wollstonecraft published controversial book

Mary Wollstonecraft (1759–1797) was born in London, England. She witnessed the abuse of her mother by an alcoholic father, who squandered the family's money. At first Wollstonecraft earned a living by sewing and teaching, two occupations then open to young women. Mostly self-educated, she began working as a translator for a publisher in 1788. Her job brought her into contact with political writers and reformers known as English Jacobins (similar to the French Jacobins, a radical revolutionary group that advocated overthrowing the monarchy and establishing a democratic form of government during the French Revolution, 1789–1799). Among them were her future husband, William Godwin. In 1790 Wollstonecraft wrote *Vindication of the Rights of Man,* in response to *Reflections on the French Revolution* by British politician Edmund Burke. Two years later she published *Vindication of the Rights of Woman,* which is now considered the most important of the feminist works of the late eighteenth century.

That same year—1792—Wollstonecraft traveled to Paris, France, to be a firsthand witness to the Reign of Terror (a period of violent mass executions of antirevolutionary suspects during the French Revolution). In 1794 she published *View of the French Revolution,* the first volume of her account of the events she had seen in France. Wollstonecraft was then ostracized for her radical political views. Around the same time she had a daughter, Fanny, with Captain Gilbert Imlay, an American merchant. (Fanny Imlay committed suicide at the age of twenty-two.) When Imlay deserted Wollstonecraft, she tried to commit suicide. In 1797 she married Godwin, then died giving birth to a daughter, Mary, who would marry British poet Percy Bysshe Shelley and write the classic novel *Frankenstein.*

1793 ▪ Madame Roland executed for activism

French feminist Madame Manon Philipon Roland (1754–1793) was always an avid reader, enjoying romantic

Although she came from an aristocratic family, Charlotte Corday supported the French Revolution.

novels and the Greek classics as a child. In 1780 she married Jean-Marie Roland, moving with him to Paris. Her husband became a prominent political figure during the French Revolution (1789–1799), serving as the king's minister of the interior from 1792 to 1793. (The French Revolution was a movement to overthrow the monarchy and replace it with a democratic form of government.)

In Paris, Madame Roland opened a salon that was a popular meeting place for revolutionary politicians and thinkers. As an outspoken feminist, she pressed for women's political and social rights. When the Jacobins (a radical revolutionary group led by Maximilien Robespierre, Georges Jacques Danton, and Jean Paul Marat) cracked down on their political opposition, they took as prisoners many prominent feminists, including Madame Roland. While awaiting trial in prison she wrote *Appeal to Impartial Posterity,* an important account of the revolution. She was beheaded on the guillotine in 1793 for a charge of treason, but actually she was killed because the Jacobins wanted to suppress feminist elements in the revolution. Madame Roland's last words were, "O liberty! O liberty! What crimes are committed in thy name!" Informed of his wife's death a week later, Jean-Marie Roland reportedly committed suicide by falling on his sword.

1793 ▪ Charlotte Corday assassinated Jean Paul Marat

Charlotte Corday (1768–1793) was born Marie Charlotte Corday d'Armont in St. Saturnin, France. Although she came from an aristocratic family, Corday was sympathetic to the French Revolution (1789–1799), a movement to overthrow the monarchy and replace it with a democratic form of government. After King Louis XVI and Marie Antoinette were executed on the guillotine, the revolution in France became more radical. On one side were the extreme leaders Maximilien

Robespierre, Georges Jacques Danton, and Jean Paul Marat. They were known as "the Mountain" because they were seated on high benches at the rear of the National Convention (the group that was writing a new constitution). As "the Mountain," these three men wielded the power in the Jacobin Club, a radical revolutionary group.

In opposition to the Jacobins were the Girondists, who advocated a more moderate approach to forming a French republic (democracy). In June 1793 the National Convention arrested and executed many Girondists. A Girondist sympathizer, Corday was horrified by the Jacobins' brutality. She went to Paris and, posing as a messenger, requested a meeting with Marat. Led into the room where he was taking a bath, Corday stabbed him after he commented that he would have all the Girondists guillotined. Corday was immediately arrested and sentenced to death. She was executed four days later. Corday's assassination of Marat inspired many paintings, poetry, and songs.

Napoleonic Code Promoted Inequality

In 1804 the Napoleonic Code removed the few gains women had made during the French Revolution and made women legally subordinate to (or placed them under the authority of) men. The Napoleonic Code was a set of laws established by Napoleon Bonaparte, the emperor of France. It allowed divorce under limited circumstances but clearly favored husbands over wives. Under the code, women could not vote, sit on juries, serve as legal witnesses, or sit on chambers of commerce or boards of trade. After Napoleon's final downfall in 1815, the restored French king Louis XVIII outlawed divorce entirely and kept the other laws in place.

1796 ▪ Joséphine de Beauharnais married Napoleon

Joséphine Tascher de la Pagerie (1763–1814) was born in Martinique, West Indies. In 1779, at the age of 16, she married the vicomte de Beauharnais, with whom she had two children. Finding Joséphine to be too unsophisticated for his tastes, Beauharnais separated from her in 1785. Joséphine then moved to Paris, where she became active in high society and eventually became the mistress of the comte (count) de Barras. In 1794 her husband (Beauharnais, from whom she was separated) was executed in the French Revolution (1789–1799; a movement to overturn the French monarchy and replace it with a democratic form of government). Josephine was imprisoned only briefly.

Two years later, Joséphine married Corsican military officer Napoléon Bonaparte in a civil ceremony. Napoléon had been promoted to brigadier general and placed in command of French Convention forces. (The French Convention was the governing body that had ruled France since the monarchy was overthrown in 1789.) Fearing a royalist (pro-monarchy) revolt, the convention ordered Napoléon to defend the country against supporters of the royal family in Europe.

Joséphine accompanied Napoléon during his invasion of Italy, but she returned to Paris as he swept to victory throughout Italy over the next year. In 1804, after the couple was remarried in a religious ceremony, Napoléon became emperor of France. As empress Joséphine enhanced her husband's power by attracting French intellectuals to their residence, Malmaison, and to the Luxembourg and Tuilleries palaces. Yet Napoléon became dissatisfied with Joséphine's inability to bear children (he wanted to start a dynasty, or ruling family), so he divorced her in 1809. Their marriage was later invalidated (declared null and void, as if it had never taken place) because a parish priest had not been present at the 1804 religious ceremony.

1800 ▪ Caroline Milhaud promoted study of society

Caroline Milhaud was a pioneer feminist and scientist in France. She believed that knowledge of the modern social sciences (including sociology, economics, political science, and geography) could correct social ills and eliminate class conflict. Milhaud supported the theory of positivism, which promoted the study of society in order to discover "positive" social laws. A member of the middle class, Milhaud conducted interviews with working women to understand their lives and to seek scientific solutions to their problems. Like other positivist reformers, she tried to repair the rift, or separation, that had developed among women of differing social classes.

1800 ▪ Maria Edgeworth published "social novel"

Maria Edgeworth (1767–1849), the daughter of British inventor and writer Richard Lovell Edgeworth (1744–1817), was born in Oxfordshire, England. In 1782 she accompanied her father to Edgeworthstown, Ireland, where she helped him manage the family estate and acted as governess to her numerous brothers and sisters. (Richard Edgeworth eventually had 14 children with three wives.) With her father she wrote books on childhood education.

In 1800 Edgeworth published her first novel, *Castle Rackrent,* which was acclaimed for its humorous yet insightful portrayal of the social class system in Ireland. The following year she wrote *Belinda.* This work received praise from such important writers as Sir Walter Scott and became famous in Europe.

Throughout her life Edgeworth was sympathetic to the plight of the Irish, who had been under British rule for 300 years. She is remembered for the assistance she gave to starving people during Ireland's Great Potato Famine (1846–1849), which was caused by a potato blight (infestation or ruination of a crop) and resulted in thousands of deaths.

"Sweet Betsy from Pike" Represents American Pioneer Women

One of the most popular songs to come out of the California Gold Rush, "Sweet Betsy from Pike," told the story of a character named Sweet Betsy from Pike County, Missouri, who traveled by covered wagon across the prairies and mountains to California. Having survived cholera epidemics (a severe gastrointestinal disease that struck large numbers of people at the same time), raids by Native American tribes, snowstorms, and the alkali water of the deserts, "Sweet Betsy" exemplified all the pioneering women of the early nineteenth century who ventured into the frontier and thrived there.

1800 ▪ Wang Zhaoyuan annotated ancient text

Wang Zhaoyuan (1763–1851) was a scholar who participated in the Kaozheng school, which flourished in China in the eighteenth century. One of the primary goals of this school was the study of ancient texts. In 1800 Zhaoyuan produced annotated editions of Han dynasty (ruling family) scholar Liu Xiang's *Biographies of Virtuous Women.*

1804 ▪ Sacajawea was guide for Lewis and Clark

Sacajawea (c. 1784–c. 1812) was born in Idaho into the Lemhi (Shoshoni) tribe of Native American people but was

Sacajawea guided Lewis and Clark safely through the wilderness, contributing to the success of an expedition that expanded American territory.

kidnapped at age ten by members of the Hidatsa tribe. In 1804 she was either purchased or won by fur trader Toussaint Charbonneau, whom she married. Charbonneau was hired that same year by explorers Meriwether Lewis and William Clark to serve as an interpreter for their expedition across the United States. Sacajawea and their two-month-old son accompanied him. As a speaker of Shoshoni and Siouan, Sacajawea proved invaluable as an interpreter. She also guided the group safely through the wilderness, contributing to the success of an expedition that expanded American territory into the Pacific Northwest.

1805 ▪ Marie Lavoisier published *Memoirs of Chemistry*

Marie Lavoisier (1758–1836) was born Marie Anne Paulze. When she was 14 her father arranged her marriage to 28-year-old Antoine-Laurent Lavoisier, who has been credited with founding modern chemistry. Antoine taught her Latin and

English, and she used these language skills to translate important scientific works from English.

Marie collaborated with Antoine on all of his experiments. Together they discovered oxygen, discrediting the then-current notion that combustion (or burning) resulted from the release of a substance called "phlogiston" (pronounced flo-JIS-ten). They also formulated the Law of the Conservation of

Matter and applied the principles of inorganic (matter other than plant or animal) chemistry to physiological phenomena (living matter). Marie used her artistic skill to illustrate their books, and she opened a scientific salon (a meeting place for intellectual exchange) in Paris.

During the French Revolution (a movement to overthrow the monarchy and establish a democratic form of government), Antoine was arrested for being an employee of Louis XVI. He was later executed. Although Marie was also imprisoned, she was not convicted of any charges. After her release from prison she wrote *Memoirs of Chemistry* (1805), publishing the book under Antoine's name.

1809 ▪ Elizabeth Seton founded Sisters of Charity

Elizabeth Ann Bayley Seton (1774–1821) was born into a wealthy New York City family, and at age 19 she married an equally wealthy man. In 1797 she founded the Society for the Relief of Poor Widows with Small Children. After her husband lost his fortune the couple moved to Italy, where Elizabeth grew interested in the Roman Catholic religion. Upon her husband's death in 1803 Seton was left with five children. Returning to the United States, she converted from Episcopalianism to Catholicism. In 1809 she founded the Sisters of Charity, the first religious order in the United States. The sisters dedicated themselves to improving the conditions of the poor and supporting parish school education.

Although she continued to raise her children, Seton became a nun and, as Mother Seton, served as the head of the order. She is credited with starting the Catholic school system in the United States. In 1975 Seton became the first American-born person to be named a saint. Her feast day is January 4.

1811 ▪ Jane Austen published first novel

Jane Austen (1775–1817) was born at Steventon, Hampshire, England, one of seven children of the Reverend George and Cassandra Leigh Austen. Educated at home with her older sister Cassandra, Austen began writing stories at an early age—primarily for the amusement of her family. Until 1800 she wrote at her home in Steventon, then continued for the next eight years at nearby Clawton. Although she had several suitors, she remained unmarried.

In 1797 Austen completed her first novel, *Pride and Prejudice,* then wrote *Sense and Sensibility* and *Northanger Abbey* two years later. But when all three works were rejected for publication, she stopped writing. In 1811 *Sense and Sensibility* was finally published, and Austen decided to take up writing once more. *Pride and Prejudice* was published next (1813), followed by *Mansfield Park* (1814) and *Emma* (1815). During her lifetime the author's name did not appear on the title page of any of her books, so she received little public recognition until years after her death.

Jane Austen's name did not appear on the title page of any of her books. As a result, she received little public recognition until years after her death.

Austen completed *Persuasion* as her health began to fail during the final year of her life. She died in 1817 and was buried in Winchester Abbey. *Northanger Abbey* was published a year later. Austen is now regarded as one of Britain's greatest novelists. Her novels have gained a wider audience due to several feature film and television adaptations, including *Pride and Prejudice* (1995) and *Emma* (1996).

1813 ▪ Laura Secord provided vital information to army

Laura Secord (1775–?) was a colonist who lived in Queenston, Ontario, Canada. In 1813, during the War of 1812 (1812–1815; an armed conflict between the United States and Great Britain), she overheard two American officers discussing military plans while dining at her house. Secord immediately began a 30-kilometer trek (nearly 19 miles) on foot from Queenston to Beaver Dams to warn a British officer named James Fitzgibbon that the Americans were planning to attack his outpost. Two days later, the Americans were ambushed by

Mississippi Supreme Court Allows Husbands to Beat Wives

The Supreme Court of Mississippi became the first state court to recognize a husband's right to beat his wife. Even though some states adopted anti-wife-beating laws in the late nineteenth century, no real enforcement policies existed. In the colonial era, a husband was allowed to punish his wife as long as he beat her with a stick no thicker than his thumb. In the early 1800s, on rare occasions when men were finally brought to court for severely beating their wives, judges routinely dismissed such cases. Until the Civil War (1861–1865), neither the government nor the courts tried to stop domestic violence.

Indians at Beaver Dams and 400 men surrendered to Fitzgibbon. Although Secord was perceived by many as a heroine, she herself received little recognition for her action. Instead, in 1828 her husband was rewarded with a series of offices in local government. When Secord was widowed in 1841 she was left penniless and taught school to earn a living. At the age of 85 she finally received a small reward from the Prince of Wales.

1816 ▪ Mary Reiby became successful businesswoman

Molly (Mary) Haydock (1777–1855) was born in Bury, Lancashire, England. Both of her parents died when she was quite young. At the age of 13 she dressed as a boy and ran away to start a new life. The young orphan was then arrested—and actually sentenced to death—for stealing a horse. When her true gender was revealed during her trial, she was instead sent to New South Wales, Australia, for seven years. In 1794 she married Thomas Reiby, and the couple established themselves as business developers. Although her husband died in 1811, Reiby continued their business, and it became quite clear that she had been the driving force behind their success. Within five years Reiby was known as Australia's first highly successful businesswoman. Her estate was valued at 20,000 pounds, and she owned 1,000 acres of land. A supporter of charities and education, Reiby opened the Bank of New South Wales in her home in 1817.

1816 ▪ Mathematician Sophie Germain won award

Frenchwoman Sophie Germain (1776–1831) was a self-taught mathematician. At the beginning of the nineteenth century many mathematicians were researching the vibration of elastic surfaces, and French ruler Napoleon ordered the Academy of Sciences to hold an essay competition on the subject. Germain submitted her first entry in 1811, but it was rejected. In 1816 she submitted another essay—this one exposing the laws of vibrating elastic surfaces by describing a fourth-order partial differential equation. Although Germain was awarded a gold medal worth 3,000 francs, she was denied membership in the French Academy of Sciences because she was a woman.

1818 ▪ Mary Shelley wrote *Frankenstein*

Mary Wollstonecraft Shelley (1797–1851) was the daughter of Mary Wollstonecraft and William Godwin. At the age of 17 she had a scandalous relationship with English poet Percy Bysshe Shelley, whom she married in 1816. Like her mother, who wrote *Vindication of the Rights of Woman* (1792), Shelley criticized male-dominated society. In 1818 she produced the novel *Frankenstein,* which was an immediate success and has since become a classic. This novel depicts Shelley's vision of a harsh and unnatural world—a male-centered world of violence. Dr. Frankenstein is said to symbolize the egoism of the Industrial Revolution. (Egoism is a philosophy that places individual self-interest above all else; the Industrial Revolution—c. 1750 to c. 1850—was a period of rapid economic change in Britain that followed the discovery of steam power.) Among Shelley's other works are the novels *The Last Man* (1826) and *Lodore* (1835), as well as poems and plays. (*Also see entry dated 1792: Mary Wollstonecraft published controversial book.*)

1821 ▪ Emma Hart Willard founded female seminary

Emma Hart (1787–1870) was born and educated in Berlin, Connecticut. After marrying Dr. John Willard in 1809, she studied geometry and philosophy, subjects that were not usually taught to women of her era. In 1814 she started Middlebury Female Seminary, a college preparatory school for girls. Willard also published her "Plan for Improving Female Education." The governor of New York recommended the plan to the state legislature and urged Willard to move her school to

Troy, New York. Named the Troy Female Seminary, it became the first privately funded school for girls in the United States.

1823 ▪ Catharine Beecher started school for women teachers

American educator Catharine Beecher (1800–1878) was born in New York. In 1823 she founded the Hartford Female Seminary. Beecher felt that education was "a true profession for women," as important as their responsibilities in the home as mothers. At her school she prepared young American women to serve as teachers in the newly settled regions of the West. Beecher did not support women's suffrage (right to vote); rather, she urged women to work together to demand that their unpaid work in the home be given the same respect as men's paid labor.

1825 ▪ Frances Wright supported emancipation of slaves

Frances Wright (1795–1852) was the daughter of an upper-class family in Dundee, Scotland. In 1818 she immigrated to the United States, where she published novels, plays, and a book on American society. Seven years later Wright and social reformer Marie Joseph Lafayette purchased 320 acres of marshy swampland in western Tennessee. There they established Nashoba, a commune (a community in which people share work) for promoting the gradual emancipation (freeing) of slaves. The Nashoba experiment lasted only four years, however, and Wright later moved to New York, where she published a socialist journal. (A socialist is an advocate of a classless society who believes in government ownership and distribution of goods and services.)

1825 ▪ Rebecca Webb Lukens was iron industry manager

Rebecca Webb Lukens (1794–1854) was the daughter of the founder of the Brandywine Rolling Mill. In 1825 Lukens became the first female manager in the American iron industry when she took over the mill after the death of her husband. In 1890 the business was renamed Lukens Mills.

1828 ▪ Ranavalona I launched coup d'etat

King Radama of Madagascar (an island in the Indian Ocean off the coast of eastern Africa) followed pro-European policies during his reign. Upon his death, his wife, Ranavalona of Madagascar, launched a coup d'etat (a violent overthrow of government) in which all of the king's relatives were murdered. To secure her hold on the throne, Ranavalona declared herself to be a man. Her method of governing contrasted sharply with that of her husband. In 1828 she repudiated (rejected; refused to accept the terms of) the Anglo-Malagasy Friendship Treaty between Madagascar and Britain. Ranavalona also reintroduced slavery as a social and economic feature of Malagasy life.

1829 ▪ Kementyna Tonska Hoffmanowa fled homeland

Kementyna Tonska Hoffmanowa (1798–1845) was born in Warsaw, Poland, which was then within the Russian empire. When the Russians attempted to wipe out the Polish language and literature, Hoffmanowa initiated activities to preserve her country's heritage. Writing numerous children's works in Polish, she took great interest in the development of Polish schools. In 1829 she married noted historian and patriot Karol Hoffman. Hoffmanowa and her husband were forced to flee Russian persecution in their native land and settle in Paris, France. A 15-volume collection of Hoffmanowa's works has gone through many Polish editions.

1831 ▪ Elizabeth Gould illustrated bird book

Artist and naturalist (student of natural history) Elizabeth Coxen Gould (1804–1841) was born and educated in England. She was a zoologist (zoology is the branch of biology that deals with animals), ornithologist (one who studies birds), linguist (one who studies language), musician, and gifted pictorial artist (illustrator). After working briefly as a governess in London, she married a poorly educated taxidermist (a person who prepares and stuffs the skins of dead animals) named John Gould in 1828. Three years later he published *A Century of Birds from the Himalayan Mountains,* whose most notable feature was the 80 color plates it contained—all painted by Elizabeth.

1832 ▪ George Sand published her first novel

George Sand (1804–1876), the pen name for Amandine Aurore Lucile Dupin Dudevant, was born in Paris, France. An illegitimate child, Dupin grew up in the French village of Nohant. Her father served under the French ruler Napoleon, but her mother was a low-born, poorly educated working woman. This combination of vastly different backgrounds sparked a rebellious streak in young Dupin. Following a brief marriage to the Baron Dudevant, she left her family for life among the intellectuals of Paris. She is remembered for blatantly defying social convention: she dressed in men's clothes, smoked cigars, and had several love affairs—the most notable being one with Polish pianist and composer Frédéric Chopin. Having taken her pen name from one of her lovers, George Sandeau, Sand published her first novel, *Indiana,* in 1832. She continued to immerse herself in the world of politicians and philosophers before settling down to stricter literary pursuits in 1848.

George Sand was the pen name for French novelist Amandine Aurore Lucile Dupin Dudevant.

1833 ▪ Lydia Maria Child wrote antislavery book

American abolitionist Lydia Maria Francis Child (1802–1880) was born in Medford, Massachusetts. Her first novel, *Hobomok,* was published in 1824. Beginning in 1826 Child served as the editor of *Juvenile Miscellany,* one of the first magazines for children in America and the forerunner of *Harper's Young People.* In 1828 she married David Lee Child. Her abolitionist works included *An Appeal in Favor of That Class of Americans Called Africans* (1833). Child also edited *National Anti-Slavery Standard* with her husband from 1841 to 1849. Her antislavery position caused both her career and her social position to suffer: she was ostracized (excluded or shunned by society, in this case, racist white society), and her books were returned to the publisher.

1835 ▪ Madame Tussaud established wax museum

Marie Groshotz Tussaud (1761–1850) was born in Strasbourg, Switzerland. At an early age she served as an apprentice wax modeler under her uncle, Philippe Curtius, in Paris, France. She inherited Curtius's museums upon his death in 1794.

During the French Revolution (1789–1799; a struggle to replace the French monarchy with a democratic form of government) Marie made death masks of the severed heads of people executed on the guillotine. Following a short time spent in prison for "crimes against the government," she married François Tussaud. In 1800, after she and her husband were separated, Tussaud moved to England with her son. She toured the country as Madame Tussaud, exhibiting life-size wax replicas of famous heroes and criminals. In 1835 Tussaud opened her famous waxworks on Baker Street in London. Later moved to Marlybone Road, the museum was destroyed by fire in 1888. It was rebuilt on the same site in 1925 and still contains some of Tussaud's own figures, including a model of Marie Antoinette (*Also see entry dated 1774: Marie Antoinette became queen of France.*)

During the French Revolution, Madame Tussaud made death masks of the severed heads of people executed on the guillotine.

1835 ▪ Harriet Jane Hanson Robinson worked in mill at age ten

Harriet Jane Hanson Robinson (1825–1911) became a bobbin tender (one who tends to spindles of yarn or thread used in making cloth) in a textile mill in Lowell, Massachusetts, when she was just ten years old. Later on she became a frequent contributor to *The Lowell Offering,* the literary magazine of the textile mill workers. Her writings took a positive tone regarding mill work and conditions. In addition to writing for the magazine, Robinson published five other works. Her memoir, *Loom and Spindle,* is considered the best book of reminiscences about the early days of the mill.

1836 ▪ The Grimké sisters lectured on abolition

Angelina Emily Grimké (1805–1879) and her sister, Sarah Moore Grimké (1792–1873), were children of a slave-owning father in South Carolina. Both converted to Quakerism (also called the Society of Friends; members of a Christian sect that promotes justice, peace, and simplicity in living) and became involved in the abolitionist (antislavery) movement in the United States. In 1868 Angelina published "An Appeal to the Christian Women of the South," a pamphlet advocating the abolition of slavery. However, many Southern postmasters destroyed copies of the work rather than deliver them.

Sarah also published extensively. Her works included "Epistle to the Clergy of the Southern States" (1827); "Letters on the Condition of Woman and the Equality of the Sexes" (1838); and a translation of French poet Alphonse Lamartine's "Joan of Arc" (1867). Sarah was silenced during a Quaker meeting for voicing her antislavery views. The experience strengthened her resolve to fight for the abolitionist cause and for a woman's right to voice her opinions.

1836 ▪ Sarah Bagley was union organizer

Sarah Bagley was born in Meredith, New Hampshire. In 1836 she took a job as a weaver in a textile mill in Lowell, Massachusetts. Disturbed by the poor working conditions—inadequate lighting and ventilation and a punishing 12-hour workday—Bagley quickly became a major figure in the fight for laborers' rights. She conducted free classes for other mill workers, promoted the ten-hour workday movement, and pressured the state legislature to hold public hearings on conditions in the textile mills.

A prolific writer, Bagley contributed many articles to workers' publications such as *The Lowell Offering* and *The Voice of Industry*. However, her submissions were usually rejected because they were critical of the factories and their owners. Bagley was a leader of the Lowell Female Labor Reform Association, one of the earliest major unions organized for working women. Under Bagley's leadership, the association purchased *The Voice of Industry* and used the pamphlet as a vehicle to provide a realistic view of factory life. Bagley disappeared from known records in the mid–1840s, possibly because of her activism and union connections. She reemerged in late 1846 as the first telegraph operator.

1836 ▪ Mary Lyon helped found Mount Holyoke Seminary

American educator Mary Lyon (1797–1849) raised the funds to found Mount Holyoke seminary in South Hadley, Massachusetts. The cornerstone for the first building was laid in the mid–1830s, and classes convened in the fall of 1837. The seminary eventually became Mount Holyoke College, the first four-year college for women in the United States. Lyon served as principal of the seminary from 1837 to 1849, publishing a number of works on women's education, including "Tendencies of the Principles Embraced and the System Adopted in the Mount Holyoke Seminary" (1840).

1837 ▪ Laura Bridgman pioneered method of teaching the blind

Laura Dewey Bridgman (1829–1889) was born in Hanover, New Hampshire. When she was just two years old, a high fever destroyed her senses of sight, hearing, and smell. In 1837, at the age of 18, Bridgman entered the Perkins School for the Blind, where she was educated by Dr. Samuel Howe. To teach her to read, Howe used a raised alphabet similar to the Braille system used today. (The Braille system consists of raised dots—imprinted on a surface such as paper, leather, or wood—that visually impaired people can learn to "read" through touch.) The first person to be taught according this method, Bridgman herself became a teacher of people who could not see, hear, or speak.

1837 ▪ Sara Josepha Hale edited Godey's *Lady's Book*

Sarah Josepha Buell Hale (1788–1879) was born in Newport, New Hampshire. When she was widowed in 1822 she

Ohio Colleges Admit Women

Oberlin College in Oberlin, Ohio, was founded in 1833. Oberlin's administrators noted that the college was "always open to all students," including women. In 1852 Antioch College in Yellow Springs, Ohio, also began to admit women.

became a writer in order to support her five children. After publishing a two-volume novel titled *Northwood* (1827), she was appointed editor of *Ladies' Magazine* in Boston, becoming the first female editor of a magazine. When the publication was bought by French publisher Louis Godey and renamed in 1837, Hale began her 40-year tenure as editor of the new magazine, which was called *Lady's Book*. Hale was also instrumental in establishing the Thanksgiving holiday, and she wrote the ever-popular children's poem "Mary Had a Little Lamb." In 1853 she published *Woman's Record,* a biography of 2,500 women from ancient times to 1850.

1837 ▪ Queen Victoria began ruling Great Britain

Alexandria Victoria (1819–1901) became Queen Victoria of England at the age of 18 upon the death of her uncle, King William IV. In 1840 she married Prince Albert of Saxe-Coborg-Gotha, with whom she had nine children, and who strongly influenced her rule of the British empire. Victoria was well known for her displays of maternal devotion: she always appeared with her children at ceremonial functions, and she set an example of virtue and good behavior for her subjects.

When Albert died in 1861, Victoria was grief-stricken, withdrawing from social activities and dressing in mourning (wearing black) for several years. In 1897 her Diamond Jubilee (50-year reign) was celebrated as a great "festival of empire." Victoria ruled for a total of 63 years—the longest reign of any British monarch. While she was on the throne Britain reached the height of its power, with industrial expansion at home (an increase in manufacturing activities) and imperial expansion abroad (the formation of British colonies on foreign soil). This period came to be known as the Victorian Era.

1838 ▪ Flora Tristan started her writing career

Flora Tristan (1803–1844) was born to a wealthy Peruvian father and a French mother in Paris, France. At age 18 she began working in a print shop and soon married the owner, André Chazal. They had three children, but in 1825 Tristan left Chazal because he had mistreated her. She traveled to England

Queen Victoria ruled for a total of 63 years—the longest reign of any British monarch.

as a "ladies' companion" and to Peru to restore her connections to her father's family. Tristan wrote a book about her travels, *Peregrinations of a Pariah* (1838), and a novel, *Méphis* (1838). She returned to Paris in 1835 to try to regain custody of her children.

After Chazal sexually abused the couple's eldest daughter, Tristan won a court custody case in 1837. The following year Chazal shot her in the back while she walked on a Paris street. Chazal was actually acquitted of all criminal charges in the case because Tristan had publicly embarrassed him with her writings. Tristan recovered from her injuries, but the doctors were unable to remove the bullet from her back.

1840 ▪ Elizabeth Cady Stanton supported suffrage

Elizabeth Cady Stanton (1815–1902) was born in Johnston, New York. When she married Henry B. Stanton, an anti-slavery reformer, the word "obey" was eliminated from the wedding vows. In 1840 Stanton began working with Lucretia Coffin Mott on the issue of suffrage (the right to vote) for women. Stanton was instrumental in the passage of an 1848 New York State law guaranteeing property rights to married women. That same year Stanton and Mott—along with Mary McClintock, Jane Hunt, and Martha Wright—organized the now-famous Woman's Rights Convention at Seneca Falls, New York. Stanton used her skills as a writer to compose the Declaration of Sentiments, which she presented at the convention. She patterned her work after the Declaration of Independence, stating that men and women were created equal and demanding that women be permitted to vote.

In 1851 Stanton began a collaboration with Susan B. Anthony. They published a weekly newspaper, *The Revolution* (1858–1860), and in 1869 created the National Woman Suffrage Association (NWSA), with Stanton as president. In 1888 Stanton and Anthony extended their efforts on behalf of suffrage for women by forming the International Council of Women. With Ida Harper, Matilda Gage, and Anthony, Stanton wrote the first four volumes of the six-volume work *A History of Woman Suffrage* (1881–1922). (*Also see entry dated 1888: Susan B. Anthony organized International Council of Women.*)

1840 ▪ Dancer Augusta Maywood toured Europe

Augusta Maywood (1825–1876), a ballerina trained in both Philadelphia and Paris, was the first American dancer to earn international acclaim. She performed at the Paris Opera beginning in 1838, and by 1840 she was dancing throughout Europe. She was also the first American woman to form her own traveling ballet company. Maywood toured the continent with her own managers, partners, decors, and costumes and was particularly popular in Italy in the 1840s and 1850s. A colorful personality, she made a fortune before retiring to a villa near Lake Como in Italy.

1840 ▪ Ernestine Rose petitioned for property rights

Ernestine Rose (1810–1892) wrote the first petition for a law granting married women the right to own property. The petition was reviewed by the New York State legislature in Albany, New York, and led in 1848 to a law safeguarding the property of married women.

1840 ▪ Nakayama Miki founded Tenrikyo religion

Nakayama Miki (1798–1887) founded the Japanese religion known as Tenrikyo. Religious from her youth, Miki devoted herself to the worship of Shinto (the national religion of Japan) deities (gods and goddesses) and to performing acts of compassion. At the age of 40 she claimed to have received a revelation from a deity and accepted its divine wishes to come under its possession. Miki felt it was her mission to give away her family's possessions to needy people.

Approximately 20 years after her initial revelation, Miki began to practice faith healing. She was the author of *Mikagura uta* ("Songs for the Sacred Dance") and the *Ofudesaki* ("Tip of the Divine Writing Brush"), both of which are considered the scriptures of Tenrikyo. Miki also taught her disciples dances to perform before God. The leaders and disciples of Tenrikyo were persecuted until after World War II (1939–1945), when the Japanese constitution defended religious freedom. Tenrikyo is an active religion today, and as its founder Miki is referred to as Oyasama ("Beloved Parent").

Elizabeth Cady Stanton helped pass an 1848 New York State law guaranteeing property rights to married women.

1841 ▪ Ann Lohman arrested for performing an abortion

Ann Lohman, known professionally as "Madame Restell, female physician and professor of midwifery," was arrested in New York City for aborting a quickened fetus (one that showed signs of life). Lohman operated a clinic in lower Manhattan, and after a sensational trial she was found guilty of violating the law. She used the exposure to expand her clinic in New York City and to open clinics in Boston and

Although she could neither read nor write, Sojourner Truth gained fame as an extremely skillful speaker.

Philadelphia. Lohman was arrested again in 1845 when one of her patients died. She was convicted and sent to prison. In 1878, when facing trial again for selling contraceptives (birth control devices), Lohman committed suicide.

1843 ▪ Former slave Sojourner Truth began mission for equality

Born a slave called Isabella, Sojourner Truth (c. 1797–1893) later gave herself a new name to represent her mission of traveling and preaching. The only thing known about her early life was her statement that she conversed with God from early childhood. Around the age of 30, Isabella escaped from her abusive owner and was sheltered by the Van Wagener family of New York State. In 1827, after the New York State Emancipation Act made her a free woman, one of her first acts was to sue—successfully—for the return of her son, who had been sold illegally to an Alabama slaveholder. She then settled for a while in a religious commune in Northampton, Massachusetts, where she met antislavery activist Frederick Douglass. For ten years, until 1843, she lived quietly but then was inspired to change her name to Sojourner Truth and begin preaching throughout the nation.

Although she could neither read nor write, Truth gained fame as an extremely skillful speaker. In 1850 she collaborated with Olive Gilbert on the autobiography of her life as a slave, *The Narrative of Sojourner Truth,* which was sold at her lectures. Truth spoke often about the connections between racial and sexual discrimination and was invited to lecture at many women's rights conventions. A particularly powerful speech she gave in 1851—now known by the title "Ain't I a Woman?"—was recounted many years later by writer and reformer Frances Dana Gage, who presided over the 1851 Woman's Rights Convention held in Akron, Ohio.

1844 ▪ Elizabeth Barrett Browning published *Poems*

Elizabeth Barrett (1806–1861) was born in Durham, England. She was educated at home by her strict father, who was proud of his daughter's accomplishments in classical Greek, Latin, and several modern languages. In 1821 she injured her spine in a fall, and by 1838 she had become an invalid. She spent most of her time in a darkened room, where she wrote poetry and love letters. Poet Robert Browning admired her *Poems* (1844), and the two began a correspondence. The writers finally met in 1845 and became engaged later that year. Although she was 40 years old at the time, Barrett feared her father's opposition to her marriage, so she and Browning wed in secret in 1846. The newlyweds traveled to Italy, where Barrett Browning's health improved, but she never saw or spoke to her father again.

The Brownings lived in a villa overlooking Florence, and in 1849 they had a son. The following year Barrett Browning published *Sonnets from the Portuguese,* a sequence of 44 sonnets about her love for Browning. The title came from Browning's nickname for her, "my little Portuguese," because of her dark complexion. The forty-third sonnet begins with the now-famous line, "How do I love thee? Let me count the ways." Barrett Browning also wrote poems protesting unjust social conditions such as "The Cry of the Children," about child labor in England.

1845 ▪ Artist Edmonia Lewis was born

Edmonia Lewis (1845–c. 1909) was the daughter of an African American father and a Native American (Chippewa) mother. Educated at Oberlin College in Ohio, she was the first black female sculptor in America. Lewis also studied in Rome and her pieces were exhibited along with works by Harriet Hosmer's group of women sculptors. She settled in Rome in the 1880s, but little is known about her later life.

1845 ▪ Mary Cassatt, artist of the family

Figure painter and etcher Mary Cassatt (1845–1926) was born in Pittsburgh, Pennsylvania. Cassatt spent most of her

Painter Mary Cassatt was noted for her moving portraits of mothers and children.

adulthood in Paris, France, where she was strongly influenced by the Impressionist movement. (Impressionist painters were very interested in how light illuminated forms and how color could recreate that illumination.) She was most famous for her paintings of mothers and children, including *Mother and Infant* and *Sarah in a Green Bonnet*.

1847 ▪ Unionist Elizabeth Flynn Rodgers was born

Elizabeth Flynn Rodgers (1847–1939) lived in Chicago, Illinois. Her husband, George, was a union iron molder. Rodgers was a homemaker and the mother of 12 children when she joined the Holy Order of the Knights of Labor. She became the first female member of that labor organization, heading the women's Local Assembly No. 1789. (The Knights recognized homemakers as workers and therefore considered them eligible for membership.) Rodgers was also one of the few women to be elected to the highest post a woman could hold in the organization—master workman. In that capacity she represented 40,000 members, both male and female.

1847 ▪ The Brontë sisters began publishing novels

Charlotte (1816–1855), Emily Jane (1818–1848), and Anne Brontë (1819–1849) were born in Thornton, Yorkshire, England, three of six children of the Reverend Patrick Brontë and his wife, Maria Branwell. The Brontës also had a son, Branwell, and two other daughters.

Life for the Brontë family was difficult: the two eldest children died while away at school. The three younger girls—Charlotte, Emily, and Anne—enjoyed writing and published poetry under the pseudonyms of Currer, Ellis, and Acton Bell respectively. In October 1847 Charlotte, as Currer Bell, published her masterpiece, *Jane Eyre*. Two months later Emily published *Wuthering Heights* in a single volume with Anne's work, *Agnes Gray*. In 1848 Anne published *The Tenant of Wildfell Hall*.

Emily Brontë died on December 19, 1848; Anne died less than six months later on May 28, 1849. In her loneliness, Charlotte completed *Shirley,* which was published in 1849. Her third work, *Villette,* appeared in 1853. Charlotte married her father's curate (assistant), Arthur Bell Nicholls, in June 1854. She died during pregnancy less than a year later.

1847 ▪ Maria Mitchell discovered unknown comet

Maria Mitchell (1818–1889) was born in Nantucket, Massachusetts, the daughter of astronomer William Mitchell. (Astronomers study objects and matter that exist outside of Earth's atmosphere.) While assisting her father in his observatory, she helped to calculate and record the altitudes of stars for the determination of time and latitude and the altitudes of moon phases for longitude.

In 1847 Mitchell discovered an unknown comet, gaining worldwide fame. She was awarded a gold medal by the king of Denmark. The next year Mitchell became the first—and until 1943, the only—woman elected to the Academy of Arts and Sciences in Boston, Massachusetts. Her later accomplishments included being appointed one of the original contributors computing data for the *American Ephemeris and Nautical Almanac,* a work that provides tables of data stating the exact locations of celestial bodies at specific points in time. In 1850 she was elected to the American Association for the Advancement of Science.

In 1848 Maria Mitchell became the first—and until 1943, the only—woman elected to the Academy of Arts and Sciences.

1849 ▪ Jeanne Déroin ran for French National Assembly

Jeanne Déroin (1805–1894) was born in Paris, France. Although married and a mother, she used her maiden name

Elizabeth Blackwell graduated at the top of her class from the Geneva Medical College of New York.

rather than that of her husband, Desroches. She was a socialist (an advocate of a classless society who believes in government ownership and distribution of goods and services) and briefly belonged to a utopian movement called the Saint-Simonians during the 1830s. (Utopists are believers in the possibility of a perfect human society; the Saint-Simonians were followers of French writer Louis de Rouroy, duc de Saint-Simon, who believed that a spirit of brotherhood should accompany scientific progress.)

In 1849 Déroin started the periodical *L'Opinion des femmes* ("Women's Opinion"). That same year she petitioned the Democratic-Socialist party to become a candidate for the National Assembly. Also in 1849 she helped found a national federation of workers' associations that included both men and women. The police suppressed the associations in 1850, and Déroin was sentenced to six months in jail for "conspiracy to overthrow the government by violence." In 1852 Déroin fled to England, where she continued her radical activities, publishing such works as *Almanack des femmes* ("Women's Almanac") in 1854.

1849 ▪ Elizabeth Blackwell, the first registered female physician

Elizabeth Blackwell (1821–1910) was born in Bristol, England. In 1832 her family immigrated to the United States. When her father died six years later, she took a teaching job to help support her eight sisters and brothers. At the same time she pursued medical studies on her own. By 1849 Blackwell had graduated at the top of her class at Geneva Medical College of New York State, becoming the world's first trained, registered female physician. After graduation, she worked in a hospital in Paris, France. Upon her return to the States, however, Blackwell was kept by other doctors from practicing her profession, so she began giving lectures on women's health that attracted a small following of interested patients. In 1853 she opened the New York Infirmary for Indigent Women and Children in New York City. During the Civil War (1861–1865; a bloody conflict that divided the northern and southern states along social and political lines) she trained and dispatched nurses to war fronts. After the war she returned to England and founded the London School of Medicine for Women.

1849 ▪ Amelia Jenks Bloomer promoted dress reform

Amelia Jenks Bloomer (1818–1894) was born in Homer, New York. After marrying Dexter C. Bloomer, a lawyer, in 1840, she wrote articles and gave lectures on women's voting rights, unjust marriage laws, and educational issues. In 1849 she started *The Lily,* a periodical supporting the temperance movement (a movement to outlaw or limit the use of liquor). In the first issues of the magazine Bloomer also endorsed (showed support for) actress Fanny Kemble, who had created a public furor by wearing "pantalettes" under a modified long dress for reasons of health and comfort. In 1851 *The Lily* continued its advocacy of dress reform by promoting an ensemble worn by Elizabeth Smith Miller, a cousin of Bloomer's friend Elizabeth Cady Stanton. Both Stanton and Bloomer adopted Miller's "short dress" and "Turkish trousers," which became known as the "Bloomer Costume."

1849 ▪ Margaret Fuller reported on Siege of Rome

Margaret Fuller (1810–1850) was born in Cambridgeport, Massachusetts, where she was educated by her father before attending a local school. In 1836 Fuller took a teaching job in Boston, where she became known for her "conversations"— cultural discussions that attracted leading reformers and intellectuals. In 1844, after editing the literary magazine *The Dial* for two years (1840–1842), Fuller went to New York City, where she served as literary critic for the *New York Tribune.* She then moved to Europe and became the first U.S. foreign correspondent when *Tribune* publisher Horace Greeley asked her to send dispatches back to the newspaper. While living in Italy in 1847 she married Marquis Giovanni Ossoli. Two years later Fuller witnessed the siege of Rome by the French Army and sent reports of the bombardment to the *Tribune*. Tragically, in 1850, Fuller, her husband, and their son drowned in a shipwreck on a sea crossing to New York City.

1849 ▪ Harriet Tubman escaped slavery

Harriet Tubman (c. 1820–1913) was born into slavery in Colchester, Maryland. In 1849 she escaped to Philadelphia, Pennsylvania, where she helped more than 300 slaves gain their freedom on the Underground Railroad (a secret system that helped runaway slaves from the South reach freedom in the North). Tubman became a famous abolitionist (antislavery activist), giving advice to John Brown as he was making plans to stage a slave revolt at Harper's Ferry, West Virginia, in 1859. During the Civil War (1861–1865; a bloody conflict that divided the northern and southern states along social and political lines) she was a spy and scout for the Federal Army, but she did not receive a pension for her service until 1897.

Index

Bold type indicates main entries
Italic type indicates volume numbers
Illustrations are marked by (ill.)

Isabel Perón (see entry dated 1974)

Gordon, Ruth *2:* **300-301**
Gould, Elizabeth *1:* **155**
Graham, Bette Nesmith *2:* **269**
Graham, Katherine *2:* **279**
Grand, Sarah *2:* **202**
Grandma Moses (see Moses, Anna Mary)
Grasso, Ella *2:* **306**
Greek mythology *1:* 5, 9
Greer, Germaine *2:* **295**
Grey, Lady Jane *1:* **85,** 84 (ill.), 86
Grey Panthers *2:* 296
Grimké, Angelina Emily *1:* **158**
Grimké, Sarah Moore *1:* **158**
Gripenberg, Alexandra *2:* **197-198**
Guanyin *1:* 49
Guggenheim, Peggy *2:* **237-239,** 238 (ill.)
Gulick, Charlotte *2:* **216**
Guthrie, Janet *2:* **314**
Guy, Alice *2:* **203**
Guyart, Marie *1:* **104**
Gwyn, Nell *1:* **115**
Gymanstics *2:* 301, 304, 352
Haiku poetry *1:* 118
Hale, Sara *1:* **159-160**
Halem Globetrotters *2:* 332
The Hammer of Witches 1: 77
Handler, Ruth *2:* **273**
Hansberry, Lorraine *2:* **271-272**
Hardy, Harriet *2:* **246**
Harold and Maude 2: 301
Harper, Frances *2:* **181**
Harris, Barbara *2:* **339**
Hart, Judith *2:* **272**
Harvard Law Review 2: 309
Hathor *1:* **3-4,** 4 (ill.), 8
Hatshepsut *1:* **7-8,** 7 (ill.)
Haughery, Margaret *2:* **184-185**
He Shuangqing *1:* **119**
Healy, Bernadine *2:* **344-345**
Hedges, Barbara *2:* **344**
Heike Monogatari 1: 60
Helen *1:* 10
Helena *1:* **30**
Héloïse *1:* **55**
Henry II *1:* 56, 58, 60
Henry VIII *1:* 81-82, 83, 85
Hera *1:* 5
Herrad of Landsberg *1:* **59-60**
Herschel, Caroline *1:* **140**
Herzenberg Caroline L. *2:* **336-337**
Hicks, Beatrice *2:* **257-258**
Higgins, Marguerite *2:* **260-261**

Hilda *1:* 39
Hildegard of Bingen *1:* **58-59**
Hill, Anita *2:* **345**
Hill, Octavia *2:* **188**
Hills, Carla *2:* **305**
Himiko *1:* **27**
Hindu religion *1:* 35
History of the Standard Oil Company 2: 209
Hitler, Adolf *2:* 239-240
Hobby, Oveta Culp *2:* **264-265**
Hobson, Laura Z. *2:* **255**
Hodgkin, Dorothy *2:* **282-283**
Hojo Masako *1:* **62**
Holiday, Billie *2:* **253,** 253
Holm, Jeanne *2:* **300**
Holmes, Phyllis *2:* **338**
Homer *1:* 9
Hon-Cho-Lo *1:* **95**
Hortus deliciarum 1: 59
Howe, Julia Ward *2:* **186**
Hrosvitha *1:* **47**
Hua Mu-Lan *1:* **32**
Huerta, Dolores *2:* **294-295**
Huguenots *1:* 91-92
Hulett, Josephine *2:* **298**
Hurston, Zora Neale *2:* **243-244**
Hutchinson, Anne *1:* **103-104**
Hypatia *1:* **31**
Ichiko, Kamichika *2:* **258-259**
Iditarod *2:* 331
The Illiad 1: 9
Inanna *1:* 5
Inkster, Juli *2:* **342**
Inquisition *1:* 64-65
Institute for the Study of Nonviolence *2:* 287
International Council of Women *2:* 198
Irene *1:* **43-44,** 43 (ill.)
Isabella of Spain *1:* **75-76,** 76 (ill.)
Isabelle d'Este *1:* **79-80**
Isis *1:* 3, 20
Islam *1:* 38
Italian Renaissance *1:* 94-95
Izumo no Okuni *1:* **95-96**
Jackson, Shirley Ann *2:* **305,** 305 (ill.)
Jadwiga *1:* **70-71**
Jamison, Judith *2:* **302**
Jarvis, Anna *2:* **216**
Jesus *1:* 21-22, 30, 52
Jingu *1:* **27**
Joan of Arc *1:* **73-74,** 73 (ill.)

McCormick, Anne *2:* **242**
McCullers, Carson *2:* **248-249,**
  249 (ill.)
McElmury, Audrey *2:* **293-294**
Mead, Margaret *2:* **232,** 232 (ill.)
Meir, Golda *2:* **293**
Mer-Nei *1:* **3**
Merian, Maria Sibylla *1:* **114**
Merici, Angela *1:* **82**
Merit Ptah *1:* **3**
Meyers, Ann *2:* **317**
Miaoshan *1:* **49**
Midwives *1:* 61, 99, 105
Milhaud, Caroline *1:* **146**
Millett, Kate *2:* **294**
Minerva *1:* 18
Ming dynasty *1:* 68-69
Minimum wage *2:* 218-219
Mink, Patsy *2:* **288**
Mins, Donna Mae *2:* **283-284**
Miriam *1:* 8
The Mirror 1: 67
Mitchell, Margaret *2:* **241-242,**
  241 (ill.)
Mitchell, Maria *1:* **167,** 167 (ill.)
Mitchell, Verne *2:* **233**
Mock, Geraldine *2:* **284**
Molza, Tarquinia *1:* **92**
Monophysites *1:* 36
Monroe, Marilyn *2:* **262-263,**
  263 (ill.)
Montagu, Elizabeth *1:* **131**
Montagu, Mary *1:* **120**
Montessori, Maria *2:* **220-221**
The Montessori Method 2: 220-221
Moodie, Susanna *2:* **182**
Moody, Deborah *1:* **105**
Moody, Helen Willis *2:* **211**
Moore, Marianne *2:* **260,** 260 (ill.)
Morandi, Anna *1:* **128**
Morisot, Berthe *2:* **191**
Morrison, Toni *2:* **347-348,** 347 (ill.)
Moses, Anna Mary *2:* **240**
Mother Teresa *2:* **315**
Mother's Day *2:* 216
Motley, Constance *2:* **290**
Motoko, Hani *2:* **203**
Moulton, Frances *2:* **245-246**
Mount Holyoke Seminary *1:* 159
Ms. 2: 302
Muhammad *1:* 38
Muldowney, Shirley *2:* **272,** 273 (ill.)
Murasaki Shikibu *1:* **51-51**
Murphy, Emily *2:* **226**

Muses *1:* 8
Muslims *1:* 90-91
My Brilliant Career 2: 206
Nakayama Miki *1:* **163**
Nakuta no Okimi *1:* **39**
Napoleonic Code *1:* 145
NASA (See National Aeronautics
  and Space Administration)
National Aeronautics and Space
  Administration (NASA)
  2: 351-352
National Dress Reform Association
  (NDRA) *2:* 183
National Institutes of Health (NIH)
  2: 343, 344
National Medal of Science *2:* 325,
  338, 340
National Museum of Women in
  the Arts *2:* 336
National Organization for Women
  (NOW) *2:* 293, 294
Nazis *2:* 239-240, 251, 254
NDRA (see National Dress
  Reform Association)
Nefertari *1:* **6,** 6 (ill.)
Neill, Ann *1:* **138**
Neith *1:* **3-4**
Nerthus *1:* **27**
Nieh Yin-niang *1:* **42**
Nightingale, Florence *2:* **184,**
  181 (ill.)
NIH (see National Institutes
  of Health)
Nihongi 1: 43
No drama *1:* 62
Nobel Prize: *2:* 208, 214, 282, 283,
  311, 315, 324, 347
Nogarola, Isotta *1:* **74-75**
Normans *1:* 52-53
Novella d'Andrea *1:* **66**
Novello, Antonia *2:* **343**
NOW (see National Organization
  for Women)
Nu jie 1: 24
Nur Jahan *1:* **102**
Nureyev, Rudolph *2:* 277
Nyad, Diana *2:* **308,** 309 (ill.)
Nyoni, Sakhile *2:* **350**
Nzinga, Mbande *1:* **100-101**
O'Connor, Flannery *2:* **261**
O'Connor, Sandra Day *2:* **322**
The Odyssey 1: 9
O'Keeffe, Georgia *2:* **228-229,**
  229 (ill.)